D0342233

Kitchen Keepsakes

recipes for home cookin'

Bonnie Welch & Deanna White

Illustrated by
Sheila Olson

Published by Kitchen Keepsakes
1289 Peakview Drive
Castle Rock, Colorado 80104

September, 1983   First Printing
December, 1983   Second Printing

For additional copies of KITCHEN KEEPSAKES, turn to the
last page for price and mailing address.

Copyright© 1983
Bonnie Welch and Deanna White
All rights reserved.
ISBN 0-9612258-0-7

Printed in the United States of America
by Mountain West Printing & Publishing Limited
Denver, Colorado

INTRODUCTION

This book is a collection of recipes that can truly be called keepsakes. They are the ones that have remained favorites in our families for years, and they stir memories of Sunday dinners, backyard picnics at Grandma's, and holiday gatherings. Our mothers and grandmothers prepared them for family, friends, branding and harvest crews.

Having been raised in different parts of the country, our favorite recipes reflect a variety of regional tastes, but whether it's Midwestern, Southern, or Texas-style, it's all down-home.

These foods are ones that we regularly cook (and have frequent requests for!), that do not require expensive or unusual ingredients, and are, for the most part, easy to prepare. Many are our adaptations of old stand-bys, some are family favorites contributed by friends, and all are delicious.

To insure that you find as much pleasure in preparation as we do, we have kitchen-tested all the recipes and edited them for clarity. We have included some menu suggestions—accompaniments we have found to be successful, and those that are capitalized are included within the book. Freezing and quick preparation ideas and tips for using modern kitchen equipment have also been included. In addition, we have included recipes you'll be proud to serve guests at parties, brunches, luncheons or dinners. But mostly, these are recipes you'll be proud to serve your family!

We hope you will find pleasure in preparing, serving, and eating the food from this cookbook, and that our keepsakes will become yours!

DEDICATION

This cookbook is dedicated to those ladies who inspired in us a love for good home cooking—our mothers and our husband's mothers:

Frances Matthews   Jean Sewald

Eileen Welch   Leona White

IN APPRECIATION

The following people were helpful in the creation of this cookbook. They willingly gave us recipes, advice, suggestions, and encouragement. We are most grateful to them.

Bonnie Adam	Kathleen Ness
Chris Bennett	Sheila Olson
Kathleen Budd	Candy Rayl
Judy Craig	Krynn Robinson
Zelda Cranmer	Cathy Sewald
Kevin Deets	Jean Sewald
Edith Eaton	Sherri Sewald
Joanie Graham	Dee Smith
Emily Grimes	Doris Smith
Sarah Lew Grimes	Charlotte Walker
Noanie Hepp	Dixie Welch
Mary Hier	Eileen Welch
Susie Howard	Kathy Welch
Ruth Jackson	Virginia Welch
Sid Kelsey	Laura Wesley
Judy Markoff	Leona White
Peggy Marvin	Gladys White
Frances Matthews	Kathy Williams

A special thank you to our husbands and children for their support.

TABLE OF CONTENTS

Appetizers
&
Beverages

APPETIZERS & BEVERAGES

SHELLFISH DIP

1—7½ oz. can minced
   clams or flaked crab
8 oz. cream cheese
½ cup sour cream
1 Tbsp. lemon juice
½ tsp. garlic salt
¼ tsp. pepper
¼ tsp. Lawry's seasoned
   salt
¼ cup green olives,
   chopped
¼ cup green onions,
   chopped
1 tsp. Worcestershire sauce

MAKES 2 CUPS
Combine all ingredients and mix well. Chill. Serve with potato chips or tortilla chips.

CHILI CON QUESO

½ lb. Velveeta cheese
½ lb. Old English cheese
1 medium onion, chopped
1—10 oz. can Ro-Tel
   tomatoes

MAKES 3 CUPS
Mix all ingredients and cook in top of double boiler for about 1½ hours. Serve in a chafing dish or fondue pot to keep warm. Serve with tortilla or corn chips.

TOM'S FAMOUS DIP

1 cup sour cream
1 cup mayonnaise
1 tsp. dill weed
1 tsp. parsley flakes
1 tsp. onion flakes
1 tsp. Beaumond seasoning

MAKES 2 CUPS
Mix all ingredients and serve with crudites, chips, or crackers.

CREAMY ARTICHOKE-CHEESE DIP

2—4 oz. cans artichoke
  hearts, partially drained
2—7 oz. cans green chilies,
  diced
1 cup mayonnaise
1 cup Parmesan cheese

MAKES 3 CUPS

Combine ingredients and pour into baking dish. Bake uncovered at 350° for 45 minutes to 1 hour. Serve warm with party ryes or club crackers. Cooking blends the flavors just right!

ENCHILADA DIP

½ onion, chopped
2 Tbsp. butter
2 lbs. ground beef
Garlic powder
1 can Mild Old El Paso
  Enchilada sauce
1 can Hot Old El Paso
  Enchilada sauce
2 pkg. dry enchilada sauce
1—8 oz. can tomato sauce
2 lb. brick Velveeta
  cheese, cubed

MAKES 6 CUPS

In a large Dutch oven, saute onion in butter. Add ground beef and season with garlic powder. Cook until onion is tender and beef is browned. Drain grease. Add enchilada sauces and tomato sauce. Stir in cubed cheese and cook over low heat 2-3 hours, stirring occasionally. Serve hot, with stone ground tortilla chips. (You can also use this to make your own enchiladas by placing a mixture of grated cheddar cheese and minced onion in a softened tortilla, rolling it up, placing it seam side down in a baking dish, and covering the whole batch of them with this meat sauce. Sprinkle grated cheese on top and bake at 350° for 30 minutes. You can get 8 enchiladas in a 6 x 9 inch pyrex pan.)

An experienced hostess will tell you that serving more than six varieties of appetizers is not necessary. Usually four cold ones and two hot ones are ample for a party.

APPETIZERS & BEVERAGES

FRESH FRUIT DIP

12 macaroons, crushed
¼ cup packed brown sugar
1 pint dairy sour cream
1 large pineapple

MAKES 3 CUPS
Crush macaroons and combine with brown sugar and sour cream. Chill several hours to soften macaroon crumbs. Do not stir again. Hollow out center of pineapple for serving dish. Fill shell with macaroon dip. Place in center of large platter. Arrange fresh fruits (strawberries, melons, bananas, grapes, etc.) around pineapple. This is good at a brunch.

GOOD 'N EASY GUACAMOLE

2 ripe avocados, peeled
⅓ cup sour cream
1½ Tbsp. packaged taco
    seasoning

MAKES 1 CUP
Mash avocados with fork. Add sour cream and taco seasoning and mix well. Serve with tortilla chips.

BUBBLY BROCCOLI DIP

2 Tbsp. butter
½ lb. fresh mushrooms,
    sliced
½ large onion, chopped
1½ stalks celery, diced
½ can cream of mushroom
    soup
1—10 oz. pkg. frozen
    broccoli, chopped
1—6 oz. tube garlic cheese
½ tsp. lemon juice
Salt and pepper

MAKES 3 CUPS
Saute mushrooms, onion and celery in butter. Cook broccoli according to package directions and drain. Combine all ingredients and warm to almost boiling. Remove from heat. Serve warm in chafing dish or fondue pot with tortilla chips or raw vegetables.

 After peeling an avocado, place the pit in the container with the fruit to keep it from turning brown.

4

APPETIZERS & BEVERAGES

SOMBRERO SPREAD

1—16 oz. can refried beans
1 pkg. taco seasoning
4 Tbsp. Pace's Picante
   sauce
1—7 oz. can green chilies,
   chopped
Guacamole
8 oz. sour cream
Black olives, chopped
Chopped green onions,
   tomatoes and lettuce
Grated cheddar cheese

MAKES 2 CUPS
Mix refried beans with taco seasoning. Layer ingredients on a dinner plate beginning with the beans. Top with chopped green onions, lettuce, tomato and grated cheese. Serve with tortilla chips.

CURRY DIP FOR RAW VEGETABLES

1 pint mayonnaise
2 tsp. curry powder
2 tsp. onion juice
2 tsp. vinegar
2 tsp. horseradish
Assorted raw vegetables

MAKES 2 CUPS
Mix ingredients well and serve with assorted raw vegetables.

DILLED CRAB DIP

1—8 oz. pkg. cream
   cheese, softened
1 cup mayonnaise
¼ cup sour cream
1-1½ tsp. dill weed
2 green onions, minced
1 beef bouillon cube,
   crushed
1 tsp. hot sauce
1—7 oz. can crabmeat,
   rinsed, drained
Assorted fresh vegetables

MAKES 2 CUPS
Beat cream cheese in medium size bowl until light. Beat in mayonnaise and sour cream. Stir in remaining ingredients except fresh vegetables. Refrigerate, covered, several hours to blend flavors. Serve with assorted fresh vegetables.

APPETIZERS & BEVERAGES

SMOKED OYSTER DIP

1—8 oz. pkg. cream cheese
1½ cups mayonnaise
4 dashes Tabasco
1 Tbsp. lemon juice
1—4½ oz. can chopped
　black olives
1—3½ oz. can smoked
　oysters, drained and
　chopped

MAKES 2 CUPS
Combine softened cream cheese, mayonnaise, Tabasco and lemon juice. Mix well. Add olives and smoked oysters. Delicious on raw vegetables and crackers.

SPINACH DIP

1—10 oz. pkg. frozen,
　chopped spinach thawed
1—16 oz. carton sour
　cream with chives
1 pkg. Ranch Style
　dressing mix
1 large round loaf of
　rye bread

MAKES 3 CUPS
Combine uncooked spinach, sour cream and Ranch Style dressing mix. Hollow out rye loaf saving pieces of bread for dipping. Spoon dip into loaf.

CARAMEL APPLE DIP

5-6 apples, cut into wedges
14 oz. caramel candy
8 oz. pkg. miniature
　marshmallows
⅔ cup cream or milk

Melt caramel and combine with marshmallows and cream. Stir until smooth. Pour into fondue pot. Dip apple sections in hot caramel mixture.

 When a recipe says "chop very fine" try grating it instead.

SWISS RYES

½ cup bacon, fried and
   crumbled
1 cup Swiss cheese, grated
1—4½ oz. can ripe olives,
   chopped
½ cup green onions,
   minced
1 tsp. Worcestershire sauce
¼ cup mayonnaise
Party rye bread

MAKES 25-30
Combine first six ingredients and mix well. Spread on party ryes. Bake at 375° for 10-12 minutes or until lightly browned.

STUFFED MUSHROOMS WITH BACON

1½ lbs. fresh mushrooms
6 slices bacon, diced
2 Tbsp. green pepper,
   chopped
¼ cup green onion,
   chopped
½ tsp. salt
1—3 oz. pkg. cream cheese
½ tsp. Worcestershire
   sauce
1 Tbsp. butter
½ cup dry bread crumbs

MAKES 25-30
Wash and drain mushrooms. Gently remove and dice stems. Saute bacon and drain on paper towel. Saute the diced mushroom stems, green pepper, and green onion in bacon drippings. Combine this with crumbled bacon, softened cream cheese, salt and Worcestershire sauce. Melt butter in pan and add bread crumbs. Brown crumbs and add to other ingredients. Stuff mushroom caps with mixture. Bake at 375° for 15 minutes. Serve hot.

QUICK STUFFED MUSHROOMS

1 pkg. Jimmy Dean sausage
2 lbs. fresh mushrooms

MAKES 35-40
Wash and drain mushrooms. Gently remove stems. Stuff each cap with raw sausage. Bake on cookie sheet in 350° oven for 20-30 minutes or until sausage is done. Serve hot.

APPETIZERS & BEVERAGES

CHEESE AND BACON HOT RYES

7 slices bacon, fried and
  crumbled
6 oz. cheddar cheese,
  grated
½-1 cup mayonnaise
1 Tbsp. Worcestershire
  sauce
1 small pkg. slivered
  almonds, toasted
1 small onion, chopped
Parmesan cheese
Party ryes

MAKES 3 DOZEN
Combine all ingredients except Parmesan cheese. Spread on slices of party rye bread. Sprinkle with Parmesan cheese and bake at 400° for 10-15 minutes.

DEVILED HAM PUFFS

1—8 oz. pkg. cream
  cheese, softened
1 egg yolk, beaten
1 tsp. onion juice
½ tsp. baking powder
Salt to taste
¼ tsp. horseradish
¼ tsp. hot sauce
24 party ryes
2—2¼ oz. cans deviled
  ham

MAKES 24
Blend together the cheese, egg yolk, onion juice, baking powder, salt, horseradish and hot sauce. Spread bread with deviled ham and cover each with a mound of cheese mixture. Place on cookie sheet and bake in 375° oven for 10-12 minutes or until puffed and brown. Serve hot. These can be made ahead and frozen. Remove and allow to thaw before baking.

WATER CHESTNUTS & BACON ROLL UPS

1 can whole water
  chestnuts
10 strips of bacon, cut in
  half
¼ cup soy sauce
2 Tbsp. brown sugar

MAKES 15-20
Combine soy sauce and brown sugar in small bowl. Mix well. Add drained water chestnuts and let marinate 2-6 hours. Wrap each in a bacon strip and secure with toothpick. Broil until bacon is done. Serve hot.

HOWDY POTATOES

2 medium baked potatoes
Oil
1 cup sour cream
2 green onions, chopped
1 cup cheddar cheese,
　grated
4 slices bacon, frled and
　crumbled
½ cup fresh mushrooms,
　sliced and sauteed
Salt

MAKES 16
Cut each potato into eight wedges leaving skins on. Deep fry potato wedges at 400° for 1-2 minutes or until golden brown. Arrange in sunburst pattern on platter. Mix sour cream, onions, cheese, bacon, salt and mushrooms and place in center of platter for dipping.

SPINACH APPETIZERS

2—10 oz. pkg. frozen,
　chopped spinach, thawed
　and well drained
2 cups Pepperidge Farm
　Herb Stuffing
4 eggs, well beaten
1 cup onion, finely chopped
½ cup butter, melted
½ cup Parmesan cheese,
　grated
½ tsp. garlic powder
½ tsp. MSG or Accent
½ tsp. pepper
½ tsp. salt
¼ tsp. thyme

MAKES ABOUT 70
Mix all ingredients and chill. Shape into balls and bake at 350° for 20 minutes. Serve hot. This would also be good as a vegetable casserole with a meal. Put all ingredients in a baking dish and bake at 350° about 30-35 minutes.

 Use pretzels to skewer your favorite cheese cubes rather than toothpicks.

VEGETABLE CRISPS

2 eggs
1 cup cold water
¾ cup flour
Dash salt
Assorted fresh zucchini,
　cauliflower, broccoli,
　onion, or mushrooms

Wash and drain vegetables. Slice zucchini and onions. Break cauliflower and broccoli into flowerets. Stem mushrooms, using both caps and stems. Combine eggs and water. Beat until frothy. Add flour and salt, and beat until well blended. Keep batter cold by setting it in a bowl of ice or refrigerator until ready to use. Dip fresh vegetable pieces or slices into batter. Deep fry at 375° until golden brown. Sprinkle with salt.

SHRIMP BALL

2—4½ oz. cans tiny
　shrimp, rinsed, drained,
　and mashed
½ cup mayonnaise or salad
　dressing
2 Tbsp. minced onion
Worcestershire sauce
　to taste

MAKES 1 CUP
Combine shrimp, mayonnaise, onion, and Worcestershire sauce. Form into a ball, or spoon into a crock. Refrigerate, covered, overnight for the best flavor. Serve with rice crackers.

MAMA WHITE'S CHICKEN LIVER PATE

3 Tbsp. butter
1 lb. chicken livers
¼ tsp. salt
¼ tsp. onion salt
1/8 tsp. pepper
1 medium onion, chopped
3 eggs, hard cooked
⅓ cup mayonnaise
Party ryes

MAKES 40
Melt butter in skillet. Add chicken livers, salt, pepper, and chopped onion. Fry over medium heat for about 15-20 minutes or until livers are done. Grind liver mixture and eggs through food grinder or in food processor. Add more salt and pepper to taste. Add ⅓ cup mayonnaise and mix well. Spread on party ryes.

BEST OF THE WEST SPREAD

¼ cup roasted unblanched
   almonds, chopped fine
2 strips bacon, fried and
   drained
1 cup Velveeta, grated
   and packed
½ cup mayonnaise
¼ tsp. salt
1 Tbsp. green onions
   or chives, chopped

MAKES 1½ CUPS
Finely chop onions, crumble bacon, and mix all ingredients together. Serve with crackers. If you have a food processor, chop almonds, bacon, and green onions first. Add other ingredients and blend well. Spread on crackers or bread rounds. This is delicious!

PARTY RYE SPREADS

HOT CHEDDAR SPREAD:
Grated cheddar cheese
Mayonnaise, enough to
   hold mixture together
Bacon bits

Mix ingredients together. Spread on party rye bread. Broil several minutes until mixture melts.

HAM SPREAD:
8 oz. softened cream
   cheese
1 Tbsp. mayonnaise
1 tsp. prepared mustard
2 Tbsp. drained pickle
   relish
Green onion, chopped
1 cup ham, ground

Mix ingredients together. Spread on party rye bread. These are easy and tasty!

APPETIZERS & BEVERAGES

HOT CRAB MINIATURES

1—7½ oz. can crabmeat, drained and flaked
1 Tbsp. minced green onion
1 cup Swiss cheese, grated
½ cup mayonnaise
1 tsp. lemon juice
¼ tsp. curry powder
1—5 oz. can water chestnuts, chopped and drained
1 tube flaky refrigerator biscuits

MAKES 30
Combine all ingredients except rolls. Mix well. Separate each roll into three layers. Place on cookie sheet and spoon crabmeat mixture on each. Bake at 400° for 10-12 minutes. Chicken can be substituted for the crabmeat.

SAUSAGE BISCUITS

1 lb. hot sausage
1 lb. sharp cheddar cheese, grated
3 cups Bisquick
Cayenne pepper or Tabasco sauce (optional)

MAKES 3 DOZEN
Have sausage and cheese at room temperature. Mix uncooked sausage with cheese and Bisquick. Roll into one-inch balls and place on a cookie sheet. (You may freeze these at this point, while on the cookie sheet. When frozen, take off the cookie sheet and put in a freezer bag.) Bake at 400° about 15-20 minutes or until brown. These may be frozen after baking, also.

JUDY'S GREEN CHILI PIE

1—7 oz. can green chilies, chopped
2 cups Monterey Jack cheese, grated
5 eggs, beaten

MAKES 2-3 DOZEN
Layer in order given in a greased 8 x 11 inch pan. Bake one hour at 325°. Cut into squares and serve hot.

APPETIZERS & BEVERAGES

PEOPLE PLEASIN' CHEESEBALLS

8 oz. cream cheese
1 cup sharp cheddar
cheese, grated
1 cup Monterey Jack or
Swiss cheese, grated
1 oz. bleu cheese
2 Tbsp. grated onion
4 drops Tabasco sauce
Parsley, nuts or paprika

Let cream cheese stand at room temperature until softened. Mix all ingredients together. Form into 1 big ball or three small ones. Roll in parsley, nuts or paprika. Serve with assorted crackers.

EASY CHEESE BALL

1—8 oz. pkg. Velveeta
cheese
1—5 oz. jar Old English
cheese
1—3 oz. pkg. cream
cheese
1/8 tsp. garlic powder
½ cup pecans, chopped
Paprika

1 LARGE CHEESEBALL
Have ingredients at room temperature. Mix the three cheeses and garlic powder together with your hands. When they are blended, shape mixture into a ball. Roll in paprika, then in the pecans. Refrigerate until ready to use.

CHEESY PINEAPPLE SPREAD

1—8 oz. pkg. cream cheese
1—8½ oz. can crushed
pineapple, drained
½ cup pecans, chopped
1½ Tbsp. green onions,
chopped
½ tsp. Lawry's seasoned
salt

MAKES 2½ CUPS
Soften cream cheese and mix with other ingredients. Place in small dish or crock; refrigerate. Serve with crackers.

 If cheese becomes dry, try soaking it in buttermilk and it will return to normal.

APPETIZERS & BEVERAGES

KATHLEEN'S CHUTNEY DELIGHT

1 cup chutney (see recipe
  in preserves section)
1—8 oz. pkg. cream cheese
½ cup chopped almonds,
  toasted (optional)

This can be served two ways. The cream cheese can be left in its original shape on a dish with the chutney poured over it and the almonds sprinkled on top, or you can soften the cream cheese and mix the ingredients. Best served on club crackers or celery.

CHERRY TOMATO HORS D'OEUVRES

24 cherry tomatoes
1—8 oz. pkg. cream
  cheese, softened
2 Tbsp. ketchup
1 Tbsp. lemon juice
1 Tbsp. horseradish
1 Tbsp. light cream
¼ tsp. paprika
Parsley
Watercress

MAKES 24
Wash tomatoes; dry on paper towels. Cut slice from each stem end. Combine cheese, ketchup, lemon juice, horseradish, cream and paprika. Mix well. Press cheese mixture through pastry bag with No. 6 star tip, making rosettes on each tomato. Decorate each with parsley. Arrange on watercress bed, sprinkle with lemon juice and refrigerate 30 minutes before serving.

CREAM CHEESE BURRITOS

16 oz. cream cheese,
  softened
¼ cup green chilies,
  chopped
½ cup pimento, chopped
½ cup black olives,
  chopped
4 large flour tortillas

MAKES 40 SLICES
Mix the first four ingredients. Spread an equal amount of mixture on each tortilla. Roll, cover and chill, seam side down. (This much can be done up to 7 days in advance.) To serve, slice into ¼ inch slices. Do not freeze.

CHOCOLATE DIPPED STRAWBERRIES

2 pints strawberries,
  stemmed and dried well
1—4 oz. Hershey's
  chocolate bar
1 large Tbsp. paraffin

Melt chocolate and paraffin in small saucepan. Dip end of strawberries in chocolate. Tip pan if chocolate is too shallow. These are so pretty to look at, so delicious, and so easy to prepare!

 When recipes call for softened cream cheese, warm it in the microwave for 5-10 seconds to soften.

APPETIZERS & BEVERAGES

CREAMY KOOLAID PUNCH

2 pkg. Koolaid (any flavor)
1½ cups sugar
1 cup powdered milk
½ gallon water
½ gallon vanilla ice cream
2 quarts 7-up

SERVES 25
Mix all ingredients. Keep cold.

ORANGE SLUSH

1 cup orange juice
1 Tbsp. honey
½ banana
4 ice cubes

SERVES 1
Blend all ingredients in a blender until slushy and frothy. This is a delicious summertime drink that is filling and nutritious.

APRIL SHOWER ICE CREAM PUNCH

2—6 oz. cans frozen
  lemonade concentrate
1—6 oz. can frozen orange
  juice concentrate
9 cups water
1 qt. lemon sherbet
1 qt. vanilla ice cream

SERVES 25
Mix fruit juices and water in punch bowl. Scoop sherbet and ice cream into punch. Stir gently.

BANANA FRUIT PUNCH

4 cups sugar
6 cups water
48 oz. pineapple juice
2—12 oz. cans frozen
  orange juice concentrate
1—12 oz. can frozen
  lemonade concentrate
5 bananas
3 qts. ginger ale

Mix sugar and water in saucepan. Heat to boiling. Cool. Add pineapple juice, orange juice and lemonade. Mash bananas by hand or in a blender. Add to above mixture. Stir well. Can be frozen at this point in milk cartons. Take out of freezer two hours before serving. When ready to serve, add three quarts ginger ale, and mix well.

APPETIZERS & BEVERAGES

SURE BET PUNCH

1 large can Hawaiian punch
1 pint pineapple sherbet
1 quart 7-Up

SERVES 15
Mix Hawaiian punch and 7-up. Let sherbet float on top.

FRUIT SMOOTHY

1 cup milk
1 cup fresh or frozen
   strawberries
½ cup pineapple chunks
½ cup plain yogurt
¼ cup instant nonfat
   dry milk
1 tsp. sugar
¼ tsp. vanilla
4 ice cubes

SERVES 2
Put all ingredients in blender and puree until thick and smooth.

BONNIE'S ORANGE JULIANA

⅓ cup frozen orange juice
   concentrate
½ cup milk
¼ cup sugar
½ cup water
½ tsp. vanilla
2 scoops vanilla ice cream

MAKES 3 CUPS
Combine ingredients in blender and blend until smooth. Can be made day before and kept in refrigerator.

HOT APPLE CIDER

2 quarts apple cider
½ cup brown sugar
¼ tsp. salt
1 tsp. whole allspice
1 tsp. whole cloves
3 cinnamon sticks
Orange and lemon slices

SERVES 8-10
Heat and mix all ingredients well. Cover and let simmer 15-20 minutes. Strain spices.

17

APPETIZERS & BEVERAGES

HOT BUTTERED CIDER MIX

1 cup soft butter or
   margarine
1⅓ cups light brown sugar
6 Tbsp. honey
2 tsp. nutmeg
2 tsp. cinnamon
2 tsp. vanilla
6 oz. rum, optional
Hot cider

Cream butter and sugar. Add other ingredients. Leave out rum if mixture is to be refrigerated. When ready to serve, add 1 tablespoon of mixture and 1 jigger of rum to each cup of hot cider.

HOT CHOCOLATE

1 cup milk
1 heaping tsp. cocoa
2 heaping tsp. sugar

SERVES 1
Combine cocoa and sugar in pan. Pour in ¼ cup milk and stir over medium heat. As it warms the cocoa will dissolve. Add remainder of milk. Top with marshmallows or whipped cream.

MEXICAN HOT CHOCOLATE

½ cup sugar
⅓ cup unsweetened cocoa
   powder
2 Tbsp. flour
1 tsp. ground cinnamon
½ tsp. salt
1½ cups cold water
6 cups milk
1 Tbsp. vanilla

MAKES 10 SERVINGS
Combine sugar, cocoa powder, flour, cinnamon, and salt in a large saucepan. Stir in cold water and bring to a boil stirring constantly. Reduce heat and simmer, stirring often. Slowly stir in milk and heat almost to boiling. Remove from heat, add vanilla. With a rotary beater or mixer, beat the mixture until it is frothy. Serve in mugs or cups garnishing each with a cinnamon stick or a dollop of whipped cream. This is an unusual and delicious holiday drink.

APPETIZERS & BEVERAGES

DADDY'S EGGNOG

4 eggs, separated
½ cup sugar
¼ tsp. salt
¾ cup bourbon
¾ cup milk
½ pint whipping cream
2 Tbsp. sugar
Nutmeg

MAKES 1 QUART
Cream egg yolks with ½ cup sugar, add ¼ teaspoon salt and beat until fluffy. Add bourbon and milk. Whip ½ pint cream, and fold into the egg yolk mixture. Beat egg whites to soft peaks, adding 2 tablespoons sugar. Fold into the mixture. Refrigerate. Sprinkle nutmeg on top.

GOLDEN WASSAIL

4 cups unsweetened
   pineapple juice
4 cups apple cider
1—12 oz. can apricot
   nectar
1 cup orange juice
6 inches stick cinnamon
1 tsp. whole cloves
1½ cups rum (optional)
Cinnamon sticks

MAKES 9 CUPS
In a large saucepan, combine juices and spices. Heat to boiling; reduce heat and simmer 15 to 20 minutes. Strain. Stir in rum and heat through. Serve with cinnamon stick stirrers. Great at holiday parties.

HOLIDAY PUNCH

3 pieces ginger
1—3 inch stick cinnamon
8 whole cloves
3-4 cardamom seeds
6 lemons
6 small oranges
1 gal. apple cider
1 qt. pineapple juice
½ tsp. salt
Rum, optional

40-50 SERVINGS
Tie spices in a bag of fine cheesecloth. Peel and cut lemons and oranges into thin slices and add to combined cider and pineapple juice. Add spice bag to this mixture and bring to a very low simmering boil. Stir as it simmers for 15 minutes, then add the salt and stir vigorously. Serve hot. May add rum, just before serving, if desired.

APPETIZERS & BEVERAGES

SPICED TEA

1 cup instant tea
2 cups Tang
2 cups sugar
1 envelope lemonade mix
1½ tsp. cinnamon
¾ tsp. ground cloves

MAKES 5½ CUPS
Mix ingredients well. Store in jar or tin. Place a heaping teaspoon in a mug of boiling water for a cup of delicious tea.

SANGRIA

1—12 oz. can Five Alive
   Fruit Punch frozen
   concentrate
2 cups water
1 cup wine, white or rose
Orange, lime or lemon,
   sliced thin

SERVES 8
Mix fruit juice, water and wine in large pitcher. Add ice and float sliced oranges, lemons, or limes in pitcher. This tasty, refreshing, summertime drink is especially good with Mexican food.

BLOODY MARYS

1—32 oz. can tomato juice
8 oz. vodka
¼ tsp. pepper
1-2 Tbsp. Worcestershire
   sauce
1 tsp. sugar
1 Tbsp. salt
Juice of 4 limes
6-8 dashes of Tabasco

SERVES 8
Mix together and serve over ice.

FROZEN DAIQUIRI

1—12 oz. can frozen limeade
  concentrate
12 oz. light rum
1-2 cups crushed ice
Strawberries, optional

SERVES 4

Place ingredients in a blender and blend until ice is slushy. To make strawberry daiquiries, add ½ pint strawberries before blending.

SKIER'S DELIGHT

1 qt. Burgundy wine
4 oranges, studded with
  6 cloves, and sliced
4 lemons, sliced
3 cinnamon sticks,
  in pieces
1 cup sugar

SERVES 4-6

Heat wine to a simmer; add fruit, spices and sugar. Stir to dissolve sugar. Cook 10 minutes over low heat. Remove fruit pieces and cloves. Serve in heavy mugs on a cold winter evening.

 Freeze fresh fruits and use them as you would a block of ice; nectarines, peaches, cherries, and grapes all freeze well.

Eggs

&

Cheese

EGGS & CHEESE

MORNING GLORY BRUNCH CASSEROLE

18 hard-boiled eggs
  sliced thin
1 lb. bacon, cooked
  and drained
¼ cup flour
¼ cup butter
1 cup cream
1 cup milk
1 lb. jar Cheese Whiz
¼ tsp. thyme (crushed leaf)
¼ tsp. marjoram
1/8 tsp. garlic powder
¼ cup chopped parsley,
  fresh if possible

SERVES 8-10

Hard boil eggs, cool and slice. (If you have an egg slicer, it saves a lot of time.) Make a cream sauce, adding flour to melted butter. Gradually add milk and cream, stirring constantly until thick. Add Cheese Whiz and stir until melted. Add seasonings, including half the parsley. In a buttered 9 x 12 inch baking dish, layer egg slices, sauce, crumbled bacon, etc., ending with sauce. Bake about 40 minutes, covered, in a 350° oven. Garnish with fresh parsley. Serve hot and bubbly. This is an exceptional brunch dish, especially when made a day ahead . . . gives the flavors a chance to blend, and the cook an extra hour of sleep! Serve it with Blueberry Muffins (also made ahead), grits, and a fresh Fruit Salad with Poppy Seed Dressing. You will never do better!

FRENCH HAM AND CHEESE SOUFFLE

3 cups cubed French
  bread
3 cups cubed cooked ham
½ lb. cubed cheddar
  cheese
3 Tbsp. flour
1 Tbsp. dry mustard
3 Tbsp. melted butter
4 eggs
3 cups milk
Few drops of Tabasco

SERVES 8

Make a day ahead. Layer ⅓ of the bread, ham and cheese in a buttered 9 x 13 inch dish. Mix flour and mustard. Sprinkle 1 tablespoon flour/mustard mixture over first layer of bread, ham, and cheese mixture. Drizzle 1 tablespoon melted butter over layer. Repeat twice. Beat eggs with milk and Tabasco until frothy. Pour over mixture and cover; chill overnight. Bake uncovered at 350° about 1 hour.

EGGS BENEDICT

4 English muffin halves
2 Tbsp. butter
4 slices of ham or
   Canadian bacon (or 8
   slices bacon, cooked)
4 eggs

HOLLANDAISE SAUCE:
2 egg yolks
2½-3 Tbsp. lemon juice
½ cup cold butter (1 cube)

1 avocado
2 Tbsp. sour cream

SERVES 4
Butter muffin halves and toast under broiler. Fry ham or bacon. Poach eggs. Put ham on muffin and top with egg.

Prepare hollandaise sauce. Combine egg yolks and lemon juice in small saucepan. Mix briskly. Add cube of butter whole, do not cut up. Cook over low heat, stirring constantly until thickened. Spoon hollandaise sauce over each serving. For an extra treat, top each egg with a spoonful of mashed avocado mixed with sour cream. Serve with hot buttered green peas for an added touch.

SUNDAY BRUNCH

1 dozen eggs
1 onion, chopped
3 Tbsp. butter
4-6 medium potatoes,
   diced small
1 lb. sausage, browned
   and crumbled (cooked
   ham or crumbled bacon
   can also be used)
1 cup sharp cheddar
   cheese, grated

SERVES 8
Brown onion in butter. Add diced potatoes, and cook with onion until tender. Layer a greased 9 x 11 inch casserole with potatoes and onions, then a layer of cooked, crumbled sausage. Mix the dozen eggs as though you were going to scramble them, and pour over mixture. Bake uncovered in 300° oven for 30 minutes. Stir every 5-10 minutes so it cooks evenly. Top with grated cheese the last 5 minutes. Do not overcook or eggs will get tough. Serve with Baking Powder Biscuits or Apple Muffins.

 When replacing dried herbs with fresh herbs, use twice the amount.

EGGS & CHEESE

OMLETTE FOR ONE

1 tsp. butter
2 large eggs, slightly
    beaten
1 tsp. water
Salt
Pepper

FILLINGS:
2-3 Tbsp. grated cheddar
    cheese
2-3 Tbsp. diced ham
1 tsp. chopped green onion
        •
3 Tbsp. Pace's picante
    sauce
        •
2-3 Tbsp. grated Swiss
    cheese
2 slices bacon, fried and
    crumbled
        •
2-3 Tbsp. sauteed
    mushrooms
2-3 Tbsp. Monterey Jack
    cheese, grated

Heat butter in small skillet or omlette pan until it sizzles. Mix beaten eggs with water; pour into skillet, making sure it covers the entire bottom of the pan. Cook over medium high heat until edges begin to set. Sprinkle the filling of your choice on one side of the omlette, then fold the other side over it. Lower heat; cook about 1-2 minutes more. Remove from pan and season with salt and pepper. Omlettes make wonderful Sunday night suppers, especially good with buttered toast and Strawberry Jam.

SAUSAGE SOUFFLE

4 eggs
2 cups milk
1 lb. sausage, browned
    and crumbled (cubed
    ham or crumbled
    bacon can also be used)
¼ cup cheddar cheese,
    grated
1 tsp. dry mustard
½ tsp. salt

SERVES 6
Beat 4 eggs with 2 cups milk, add other ingredients. Pour into greased 10 x 8½ x 2 inch casserole dish. Bake for 45 minutes at 350°, covered with foil, and 15 minutes at 325° uncovered. Serve with Cinnamon Rolls and orange slices dusted with powdered sugar and fresh mint leaves.

HAM AND EGG PIE

4 large eggs, beaten
¼ tsp. pepper
¼ tsp. baking powder
½ cup milk
2 cups cooked ham, cubed
1 cup grated cheddar
  cheese
1—9 inch pastry pie shell,
  unbaked

SERVES 6
Preheat oven to 425°. Beat eggs slightly. Add remaining ingredients and mix well. Pour into unbaked pie shell. Bake for 35 minutes or until inserted knife comes out clean. Serve hot or cold.

CHIPPED BEEF AND EGGS

3 Tbsp. butter
¼ cup onion, chopped
¼ cup celery, sliced
2 ½ oz. sliced processed
  beef, torn into pieces
3 Tbsp. flour
2¼ cups milk
¼ tsp. dried leaf basil
Dash of Tabasco
Salt and pepper to taste
6 eggs, hard-cooked, sliced
Toast triangles or patty
  shells for 6
  (in the frozen food section
  of the supermarket)

SERVES 6
Melt butter in large skillet. Add onion and celery and cook over low heat until tender. Add chipped beef and heat. Blend in flour. Remove from heat and stir in milk, Tabasco, and basil. Return to heat and stir over low heat until mixture thickens and boils. Add eggs and heat through. Serve over toast triangles or in patty shells.

HAM STRATA

2—10 oz. pkg. frozen,
  chopped broccoli
12 slices bread, edges
  trimmed
1½ cups cheddar cheese,
  grated
4 cups ham, diced
6 eggs
3 cups milk
½ tsp. salt
¼ tsp. dry mustard
1 Tbsp. onion flakes

SERVES 6
Cook broccoli according to package directions. Drain well. Butter a 9 x 13 inch casserole dish. Layer bottom with bread slices, grated cheese, ham, and chopped broccoli. Beat eggs and add milk, salt and mustard. Mix well and pour over layered mixture. Sprinkle with onion flakes. Refrigerate 6-8 hours or overnight. Bake, uncovered, one hour and 20 minutes at 325°.

EGGS & CHEESE

DEVILED EGGS

5 hard-boiled eggs
½ tsp. salt
¼ tsp. prepared mustard
4 tsp. mayonnaise
1 tsp. vinegar
Paprika or chopped parsley

MAKES 10
Halve shelled, cooled hard-boiled eggs lengthwise. Remove yolks and mash; add remaining ingredients and whip until smooth and fluffy. Heap into whites and sprinkle with paprika or chopped parsley.

EGG FU YONG

7 eggs
1—8 oz. can
   water chestnuts, sliced
1 cup small shrimp
1 cup bean shoots
½ green pepper, diced
⅓ onion, diced
1 Tbsp. salad oil
2-3 Tbsp. soy sauce

SAUCE:
¼ cup water
2 Tbsp. cornstarch
2 cups beef bouillon
2 Tbsp. soy sauce

SERVES 4
Beat eggs in bowl. Add water chestnuts, shrimp, bean shoots, pepper, and onion. Mix well. Pour 1 tablespoon oil in skillet and warm. Fill bottom of skillet with 1½-2 cups mixture. With spoon, spread vegetables out evenly around skillet. Cook slowly until egg mixture starts to firm and bottom is slightly golden. When egg mixture starts to set, cut it into four sections with spatula and turn each. Brown other side and serve hot with sauce spooned over top. Sprinkle with soy sauce.

To make sauce, combine cornstarch and water in small saucepan. Add beef bouillon, then soy sauce. Heat and stir until sauce is thick and smooth.

 When hardboiling eggs, put a heaping teaspoon of salt in the water to prevent the shells from cracking.

SEAFOOD QUICHE

1—9 inch pastry shell,
  unbaked
2 Tbsp. green onion,
  minced
2-3 Tbsp. butter
1 cup cooked crab, lobster
  or shrimp
3 eggs
1 cup cream
¼ tsp. salt
Pepper
¼ cup Swiss cheese,
  grated

SERVES 4-6
Saute onions in butter. Add fish and cook 2 minutes more. Beat eggs, cream and seasoning. Add cheese, fish and onion. Mix well. Pour into pastry shell and bake at 375° for 25-30 minutes.

PARMESAN QUICHE

1—10 in. cooked pie shell
4 Tbsp. Parmesan cheese,
  grated
½ lb. bacon, fried and
  crumbled
2 whole eggs plus 2 yolks
1 tsp. Dijon mustard
1 tsp. dry mustard
½ tsp. salt
1/8 tsp. cayenne pepper
⅓ cup strained bacon fat
½ cup grated Parmesan
  cheese
2½ cups scalded heavy
  cream
½ lb. bacon, fried
  and crumbled (for
  topping)
Chopped parsley

SERVES 6
Fill pie crust with 4 tablespoons Parmesan cheese and ½ pound bacon pieces. In a bowl, mix eggs and egg yolks; stir in mustards, salt, pepper, bacon fat and the ½ cup Parmesan cheese. Add cream and stir well. Pour mixture into pie crust and bake at 350° for 25 minutes. During last five minutes of baking, scatter the other ½ pound bacon pieces on top. Garnish with chopped parsley.

 To prevent a quiche or pumpkin pie crust from becoming soggy, partially bake the pastry shell in a 425° oven for 15 minutes. Brush lightly with beaten egg white or yolk and return to oven for 2 minutes. Pour the filling into the pastry shell just before baking.

Soups

&

Sandwiches

SOUPS & SANDWICHES

ASPARAGUS WITH CREAM CHEESE

1—10 oz. pkg. frozen
   asparagus, cut into
   1-inch pieces
4 cups regular strength
   chicken broth
Salt
2—3 oz. pkg. cream cheese

SERVES 6
Combine asparagus and broth in saucepan, bring to a boil, and simmer gently for 10 minutes. Add salt to taste. Cut cream cheese into ½ inch cubes and place in each soup bowl. Pour hot asparagus and broth over cream cheese and serve. This is an unusual and tasty first course soup!

BEER CHEESE SOUP

1 stalk celery, chopped
1 carrot, chopped
1 onion, minced
2 Tbsp. butter
½ cup flour
3 cans chicken broth
5 cans cheddar cheese
   soup, undiluted
1 tsp. dry mustard
6 medium potatoes, pared,
   boiled, and diced (or less
   according to your taste)
1 can beer, flat
Fresh cut broccoli, optional
Fresh cut cauliflower,
   optional

SERVES 10
In large soup pot, saute celery, carrot, and onion in butter. Blend together flour and 1 can chicken broth. Add to sauteed vegetables and stir constantly until thickened. Mix in the remaining chicken broth, cheddar cheese soup, dry mustard and potatoes. Stir well. Add flat beer. Cook over low heat, covered, for ½ hour. Add broccoli or cauliflower and cook an additional 20 minutes. This is tasty with big fat submarine sandwiches for a large crowd, or as a first course with steamed shrimp.

BROCCOLI SOUP

2—10 oz. pkg. frozen
   broccoli
¼ cup onion, chopped
2 cups chicken broth
2 Tbsp. butter
1 Tbsp. flour
1½ tsp. salt
Dash pepper
2 cups half and half

SERVES 6

In medium pan, combine onion, chicken broth and broccoli. Bring to boil, simmer for 10 minutes or until broccoli is tender. Puree in blender until very smooth. Melt butter in pan, add flour, salt and pepper. Slowly stir in half and half. Add broccoli puree and cook, stirring constantly until it bubbles.

CREAM OF CARROT SOUP

½ cup cooked rice
4 large carrots (about
   1 lb.), sliced
1 medium onion, chopped
1 small stalk celery,
   chopped (with leaves)
2 tsp. chicken bouillon
   granules
1-1½ cups water
1 tsp. salt
White pepper
¾ cup cream

SERVES 6

Place carrots, onion, and celery in saucepan with water and bouillon. Bring to boil, cover, reduce heat; simmer 15 minutes or until carrots are tender.

When vegetables are tender, drain most of the liquid into a cup and save. Puree vegetables and rice in food processor or blender until smooth. Add salt and pepper, and with machine running, add reserved broth. Return soup to pot. If serving immediately, whisk cream into soup, adjust the seasoning, and heat but don't boil. If serving later, refrigerate without cream and add just before reheating. (If you like cold soups, this one will work beautifully. Add cream to hot soup and chill.)

SOUPS & SANDWICHES

CHICKEN AND DOUGHIES

1 small chicken, stewed, deboned, and cut up
½ tsp. salt
½ tsp. pepper
¼ tsp. onion salt
¼ tsp. poultry seasoning
2 tsp. chicken bouillon granules
2 eggs
1½ cups flour

SERVES 6

Cook chicken in 1 quart water which has been seasoned with salt, pepper, onion salt and poultry seasoning. Remove chicken from broth, saving broth. Debone and cut up chicken. Return chicken to broth. Add bouillon and enough water to have 1½ quarts liquid. In bowl, beat eggs with fork. Add flour and work dough with fingers only until all the flour is moistened. (Do not overwork dough.) Bring chicken broth to a boil and drop dough into chicken soup. Break up with fingers as you drop it to make marble size pieces. Let simmer 15 minutes. Season to your liking.

CLAM CHOWDER

1 cup onion, chopped
½ cup salt pork or bacon, diced
½ cup butter
1 cup raw potatoes, diced fine
½ cup water
2 Tbsp. flour
2 cups milk
1 cup cream
2 cups clams, canned, frozen, or fresh

SERVES 6

Saute onion and salt pork or bacon in the butter until tender but not brown. Add potatoes and water and cook until potatoes are soft. Add flour, cook 2 minutes. Add milk and simmer 5 minutes, stirring constantly. Stir in cream and clams and heat through.

 If you over-salt your soup, de-salt it by slicing a raw potato into it. Boil for a short time, then remove the potato.

SOUPS & SANDWICHES

CORN CHOWDER

2 Tbsp. bacon fat
¼ cup butter
3 large onions, chopped
¼ green pepper, diced
8 medium potatoes, peeled
  and diced
4 cups milk
2 cups whipping cream
5 cups fresh corn kernels,
  or frozen kernels, cooked
¼ cup minced parsley
½-1 tsp. nutmeg
1 tsp. salt
½ tsp. pepper
¼ cup butter
6-8 slices bacon, fried
  crisp and crumbled

SERVES 12

Melt ¼ cup butter and bacon fat in skillet. Add onion and saute over medium heat until tender. Add green pepper and saute 2-3 minutes. Remove from heat. Cook potatoes in boiling water until tender. Drain well. Combine milk and cream in large saucepan and heat slowly. When warm, add all ingredients except ¼ cup butter and bacon. Bring to simmer; remove from heat and let stand at least 3 hours to thicken. Before serving, warm soup. Stir in remaining butter. Thin with milk if desired. Garnish each bowlful with crumbled bacon.

LENTIL SOUP

2 cups ham, cubed
2 cups lentils, washed
  thoroughly
5 cups hot water
1 stalk celery, chopped
1 medium onion, chopped
1 bay leaf
1/8 tsp. garlic powder
2 tsp. salt
1/8 tsp. pepper

SERVES 6

Combine all ingredients and simmer for 2 hours. Remove bay leaf. Puree in a food processor or blender. This makes a thick, hearty soup. Served with fruit and cheese, it makes a delicious winter meal.

SOUPS & SANDWICHES

CREAM OF MUSHROOM SOUP

1 lb. fresh mushrooms,
  sliced
8 green onions, including
  tops, sliced
5 cups chicken broth
¼ lb. butter
7 Tbsp. flour
½ cup dry sherry
¼ tsp. nutmeg
1 pt. heavy cream

SERVES 8
Place mushrooms in saucepan. Cook covered, over medium heat until nearly dry. Add green onions and cook until dry. Add 2 cups chicken broth. Remove from heat. In heavy 3 quart saucepan, melt butter. Add flour to make a paste, and cook, stirring over medium heat 2-3 minutes. Add vegetables in broth to butter and flour. Add remaining broth. Bring to boil, then reduce heat and simmer 20 minutes. Add sherry and simmer 10 minutes. Remove from heat. Cool 5 minutes. Whisk in cream and nutmeg and heat through. Do not boil.

QUICK MUSHROOM SOUP

1½ lbs. fresh mushrooms,
  sliced
½ cup butter
1 tsp. chicken bouillon
¼ cup water
1 pt. milk
1 pt. cream
1 tsp. salt
1 Tbsp. butter
1 Tbsp. flour

SERVES 4
Saute mushrooms in melted butter. Mix chicken bouillon with water. Pour over mushrooms; let simmer 1 minute. Combine this mixture with milk, cream and salt in a saucepan. Melt 1 tablespoon butter in a cup and add 1 tablespoon flour to make a paste. Stir into soup. Simmer 15-20 minutes.

SOUPS & SANDWICHES

FRENCH ONION SOUP

4 yellow onions, thinly
   sliced
4 Tbsp. butter
1 qt. beef stock
1½ cups croutons
   (buttered, toasted, and
   cubed French bread)
2 cups grated Swiss
   cheese
½ cup grated Parmesan
   cheese

SERVES 4
Melt butter in skillet. Saute onions until slightly brown. Add onions to beef broth in saucepan. Simmer slowly for 10 minutes. Pour into bowls. Place croutons on top of each bowlful, and either sprinkle Parmesan cheese on top and serve immediately, or cover croutons with Swiss cheese, then Parmesan and bake, covered, at 325° for 15 minutes. Uncover and bake another 10 minutes. Either way is delicious!

CHRISTMAS EVE OYSTER STEW

½ cup butter
2 pts. fresh or canned
   oysters
1 pt. cream
1 qt. milk
1½ tsp. salt
Pepper to taste

SERVES 10
Melt butter in skillet; add oysters. Cook over low heat for 10 minutes. Combine oysters and butter with other ingredients in large saucepan. Simmer, stirring occasionally, for 20 minutes. Reheat before serving. Make this specialty soup a Christmas Eve tradition —it deserves it!

HEARTY POTATO SOUP

6 potatoes, medium to large
2 slices onion, chopped
1 qt. boiling water
1 tsp. salt
¼ cup butter
1 Tbsp. flour
1 qt. milk
1 Tbsp. parsley

SERVES 6
Dice potatoes, or chop in food processor or food chopper. Cook in boiling salted water until mixture becomes thick and potatoes are soft. In large pan, melt butter, add flour, stir until smooth. Add milk, and stir constantly over medium heat, until thickened and smooth. Add potato mixture and chopped parsley. Serve hot.

SOUPS & SANDWICHES

ROCKY MOUNTAIN SOUP

6 slices bacon, diced
½ cup onion, chopped
2 cloves garlic, crushed
2 cans Ranch-style beans
½ cup rice, cooked
1—8 oz. can stewed
   tomatoes
2 tsp. salt
Dash of pepper and
   paprika
4 cups water

MAKES 6 CUPS
Fry diced bacon in saucepan. Drain. Saute onions and garlic in bacon fat until onions are golden. Add remaining ingredients and simmer 1-1½ hours to allow flavors to blend. Add water as necessary while cooking.

SAUSAGE SOUP

1 lb. bulk sausage
1 cup water
1 medium potato, diced
1 onion, chopped
1 bay leaf
1 tsp. liquid smoke
½ tsp. pepper
½ tsp. summer savory
1—10 oz. pkg. frozen
   mixed vegetables
⅓ cup water
1 tsp. sugar
2 cans cream of chicken
   soup
1 can cream of mushroom
   soup
1 can cream of celery soup
1 soup can milk
½ cup butter
⅔ cup Velveeta cheese,
   grated

SERVES 6-8
Crumble sausage in frying pan and cook until done. Drain fat. In large saucepan mix sausage, water, potato, onion, bay leaf, liquid smoke, pepper and summer savory. In small saucepan, cook the frozen vegetables, water and sugar until they are tender. Pour mixed vegetables into large saucepan, then add remaining ingredients. Stir until well blended and simmer until the potatoes are tender and flavors blended, about 30 minutes. Kids like this soup.

HOMEMADE VEGETABLE SOUP

1 beef soup bone
2 qts. water
2 bay leaves
1 Tbsp. salt
Pepper to taste
3 stalks celery, sliced
3 large carrots, peeled
  and sliced
4 medium potatoes, pared
  and chopped
2—1 lb. cans whole peeled
  tomatoes
⅓ cup barley
1 large onion, chopped

SERVES 10-12
Place soupbone in large Dutch oven and cover with water. Add bay leaves. Simmer 2 hours. Remove the soup bone and give it to the dog! Let stock cool and skim fat. Add remaining ingredients and simmer 2 more hours. Adjust seasoning. This soup is really better the day after it is made, as the flavors have blended by then. Peas, green beans, corn, or other vegetables can be added to suit your taste.

MOM'S HOT CRABMEAT SANDWICHES

12 slices bread, crust
  removed
1—7 oz. can crabmeat,
  rinsed and drained
1 cup sharp cheese, grated
Onion powder
3 eggs, beaten until frothy
3 cups milk
½ tsp. salt
1 cup sharp cheese, grated
1 can cream of mushroom
  soup

SERVES 6
Butter 6 slices of bread, and lay in bottom of 9 x 11 buttered Pyrex pan. Spread crabmeat on each piece of bread, then cheese. Sprinkle with onion powder, and top with other 6 slices of bread. Mix eggs, milk and salt. Pour over bread mixture and top with 1 cup cheese. Cover. Let stand in refrigerator overnight. Bake 1 hour, uncovered, at 350° and serve with cream of mushroom soup, heated and undiluted on top. This is really delicious and makes a nifty luncheon dish.

SOUPS & SANDWICHES

CARAWAY CRABMEAT SANDWICH

½ lb. mushrooms, sliced
1 Tbsp. butter
6½ oz. can crabmeat,
   drained and flaked
4 green onions, sliced
1 tsp. caraway seeds
Mayonnaise
8 slices bacon, cooked
   and crumbled
8 slices cheddar cheese
8 Kaiser rolls, split

SERVES 8
Saute mushrooms in butter. Combine mushrooms with crabmeat, onions, bacon and caraway seeds and enough mayonnaise to moisten. Spread crabmeat mixture on half of a roll, top with cheese slice, then other half of roll. Cover and bake at 350° for 7 minutes or until cheese melts.

CHEESE BLINTZES

1½ lb. loaf sliced white
   bread, crusts removed
8 oz. cream cheese
1 egg yolk
¼ cup sugar
2 Tbsp. minced onion
½ cup butter, melted
Paprika

MAKES 28
Beat together cream cheese, egg yolk, sugar and onion. Roll bread paper thin between wax paper with rolling pin. Place 1 tablespoon cream cheese mixture on each slice, spread and roll up. Cut in half. Roll in melted butter. Place on waxed paper, seam side down, for half hour to absorb butter. Can be refrigerated or frozen at this point. To freeze, place in freezer uncovered and separated for 1 hour, then store in plastic bag. Bake at 400° for 10 minutes or until lightly browned. Sprinkle with paprika and serve warm. These are delicious luncheon sandwiches. You can also slice them and serve as appetizers.

HOT HAM SANDWICHES

12 Kaiser rolls, split
1—8 oz. tub butter
  or margarine
2 Tbsp. poppy seeds
4 Tbsp. chives
4 Tbsp. prepared mustard
2-3 lbs. ham, sliced very
  thin
24 slices Swiss cheese

MAKES 12 SANDWICHES
Mix butter, seeds, chives and mustard. Spread on buns. Place a slice of cheese on each side of bun and ham in the middle. Wrap in heavy foil. At this point you may either freeze the sandwiches, or bake them. Bake at 375° about 20 minutes if thawed, 45 minutes if frozen. These are great to make ahead and pull out 2-3 at a time. Double the recipe if you have the freezer space.

HAM AND PIMENTO SANDWICH

2 slices bread, spread with
  Durkee's Sandwich
  Spread (can use your
  choice of mustards or
  mayonnaise)
1 slice ham (¼ inch)
1 slice pimento
1 egg, beaten
½ cup milk
Dash salt
Corn flakes, crushed
Butter, melted

MAKES 1
Make a sandwich of ham, pimento, and bread. Dip it in a mixture of egg, milk and a little salt. Roll in corn flakes and fry in butter. Rich but good!

SOUPS & SANDWICHES

HAM SALAD SANDWICH

1 cup ham, cooked and
  ground
1-2 sweet pickles, chopped,
  or 2 Tbsp. pickle relish
1 Tbsp. onion, chopped
¼-⅓ cup mayonnaise
¼ cup celery, chopped
  (optional)
2-3 eggs, hard cooked,
  chopped fine (optional)

MAKES 6
Combine all ingredients and spread
on slices of bread. Try substituting
tuna, ground roast beef, additional
chopped hard-boiled eggs, or ground
chicken for the ham.

MARCO POLOS

6 English muffin halves
1 lb. thinly sliced ham
1 lb. thinly sliced turkey
½ onion, sliced thin
1 tomato, sliced
1 or 2—10 oz. pkgs.
  broccoli, cooked and
  drained

CHEESE SAUCE:
3 Tbsp. butter
3 Tbsp. flour
2 cups milk or
  half and half
1-1½ cups cheddar
  cheese, grated
½ tsp. salt
Paprika

MAKES 6 SANDWICHES
Butter each muffin half and arrange on
a cookie sheet. Broil to toast. On each
muffin, arrange ham slice, turkey,
onion, tomato and 1-2 stalks broccoli.

To make sauce, melt butter in
saucepan, stir in flour, then milk, stirring until thickened. Add cheddar
cheese and salt; stir until melted. Pour
hot cheese sauce over warmed sandwiches (warm 10 minutes in a covered pan at 325°), then sprinkle with
paprika. (Sandwiches can also be
heated in the microwave after the
cheese sauce has been poured over
them.) These are a real quick whole-
meal sandwich that are great for drop-
in guests.

 *A pastry blender will chop hard-boiled eggs and tuna quickly
and finely for salads and sandwiches.*

FRENCH BREAD AND MEAT SANDWICH

1 loaf French bread
4 Tbsp. butter, melted
Garlic salt
1 lb. ground beef
3 Tbsp. soy sauce
1 Tbsp. chili powder
4 Tbsp. tomato paste
1 tsp. basil
2 slices chopped onion
1 lb. can dark red
   kidney beans
5 Tbsp. sour cream
1 Tbsp. chili powder
1 slice onion, chopped
1 cup cheddar cheese,
   grated

SERVES 6-8
Cut off top ⅓ of loaf of French bread. Hollow out inside of both sides, saving the bread for crumbs. Brush inside with melted butter and garlic salt. Brown hamburger; drain fat. Add soy sauce, chili powder, tomato paste, basil, and onion. Heat through. In separate bowl, mix beans, sour cream, chili powder, and onion. Place meat in bread shell, pile the bean mixture on top. Sprinkle with cheese. Replace top of bread loaf, place in foil wrapping, and bake at 350° 30-45 minutes. Slice to serve.

GLORIFIED HAMBURGERS

1 cup cabbage, chopped
½ cup carrots, shredded
¾ tsp. salt
¼ tsp. oregano
1/8 tsp. pepper
½ cup onion, chopped
1 Tbsp. water
1½ tsp. Worcestershire
   sauce
1 lb. hamburger, cooked
   and drained
4 Pita breads

SERVES 4
Combine all ingredients except beef and pitas in saucepan. Cook until vegetables are tender. Add meat and heat through. Fill pita bread with mixture; wrap each in foil and bake 15 minutes at 350°.

SOUPS & SANDWICHES

SLOPPY JOES

1 lb. ground beef
1 medium onion, chopped
3 Tbsp. ketchup
3 Tbsp. mustard
1 Tbsp. Heinz 57
   steak sauce
6 hamburger buns

SERVES 6
Brown meat and onion until onion is tender; drain fat. Add other ingredients and heat through. Serve on hamburger buns.

FRENCH DIP

Prime Rib roast, sliced thin
1 pkg. Au Jus mixture
Small French rolls

Layer thin slices of left-over prime rib on split roll. (Also good to spread sour cream and horseradish on roll.) Prepare Au Jus according to package directions. Heat Au Jus to boiling then pour into bowl for dipping sandwiches.

REUBENS

8 slices rye bread
⅓ cup mayonnaise
½ lb. sliced Swiss cheese
½ lb. sliced cooked
   corned beef
1—1 lb. can sauerkraut,
   drained
Butter

SERVES 4
Spread mayonnaise on slices of bread. Arrange cheese, corned beef and warm sauerkraut on slices. Butter outside side of bread, toast in skillet over low heat on both sides. Cover skillet with lid while toasting.

FRENCH BREAD PIZZA

1 loaf French bread
1 can pizza sauce
¾ lb. mozzarella cheese, grated
1 lb. Italian sausage (or topping of your choice), cooked and crumbled

SERVES 4
Cut bread lengthwise, top with sauce, then cheese, then sausage. Bake in 350° oven until thoroughly warmed, and cheese begins to bubble and brown, about 15 minutes.

ITALIAN SAUSAGE SANDWICH

4 small French rolls
2 lb. Italian sausage
2 cups spaghetti sauce

SERVES 4
Cut sausage into 4-inch lengths and fry slowly until done. Split the rolls lengthwise, put sausage on them, and top with warmed spaghetti sauce. Good and fast sandwich.

 To freshen stale pototo chips, crackers, etc., microwave 16 ounces for 30-45 seconds on high.

Breads

BREAD

APPLE BREAD

½ cup shortening
1 cup sugar
2 eggs, beaten
1 cup coarse ground
   apples
1 Tbsp. orange rind
2 cups flour
1 tsp. soda
½ tsp. salt
2 Tbsp. buttermilk
1 tsp. vanilla
½ cup nuts, chopped

MAKES 1 LOAF
Cream shortening, sugar, and eggs until fluffy. Stir in apples and orange rind. Sift dry ingredients and add alternately with buttermilk. Stir in vanilla and nuts. Bake in greased loaf pan at 350° for about 1 hour. Delicious!

APRICOT BREAD

2 cups sugar
1 cup vegetable oil
3 eggs
2 small jars apricot/tapioca
   baby food
1½ tsp. baking powder
½ tsp. salt
2 cups flour
1 tsp. cinnamon
1 cup chopped nuts

MAKES 2 LOAVES
Beat the sugar, oil and eggs well. Add the apricots and mix well. Sift dry ingredients and add to apricot mixture. Stir in chopped nuts. Bake in greased and floured loaf pans. Place in cold oven and turn to 350°. Bake for about 1½ hours.

BANANA BREAD

1 cup sugar
4 Tbsp. butter
1 egg
1 cup mashed bananas
1½ cup flour
½ tsp. soda
½ cup chopped nuts

MAKES 1 LOAF
Cream sugar and butter, add egg and beat until smooth. Add all other ingredients mixing well. Bake in greased and floured loaf pan for 50-60 minutes at 350°.

CHERRY BREAD

¾ cup sugar
½ cup butter or margarine
2 eggs
1 tsp. vanilla
¼ tsp. almond extract
2 cups flour
1 tsp. baking soda
½ tsp. salt
1 cup buttermilk
1 cup nuts, chopped
  (pecans or walnuts)
1—10 oz. jar maraschino
  cherries, chopped (save
  juice)

FROSTING:
1 cup powdered sugar
3 tsp. melted butter
Maraschino juice

MAKES 2 SMALL LOAVES
Cream sugar, butter, eggs, vanilla and almond extract. Mix until fluffy. Mix dry ingredients and add alternately with the buttermilk, ending with flour. Stir in chopped nuts and cherries. Pour into greased loaf pans and bake at 350° for 55-60 minutes. When cool, frost with cherry frosting. This bread is particularly festive at holiday time.

To make frosting, combine sugar and butter. Add maraschino juice, until it's the right spreading consistency for icing. A little red food coloring added to icing makes it prettier.

 Always chill fruit breads for easier slicing.

BREAD

DATE AND NUT BREAD

1 Tbsp. butter
1 scant cup sugar
2 eggs, well beaten
2 cups flour
1 tsp. salt
1 tsp. baking powder
1 tsp. baking soda
1 cup boiling water
1 cup dates, chopped
1 cup nuts, chopped

MAKES 1 LOAF

Cream butter and sugar. Add well-beaten eggs, flour, salt and baking powder. Mix well. Dissolve 1 teaspoon baking soda in 1 cup boiling water. Pour this over chopped dates and nuts. Stir well and add to flour mixture. Pour into greased loaf pan and bake 30 minutes at 400°; then lower temperature to 300° and bake another 20-30 minutes. This recipe was sent to a Colorado cook in the 1920's from her American friend living in Peking, China. It is delicious and it NEVER fails. Serve it with a meal, or slice it, spread with thinned cream cheese, and serve as an appetizer.

PINEAPPLE CARROT BREAD

3 eggs
1½ cups salad oil
2 cups sugar
2 cups grated raw carrots
1 small can crushed
   pineapple with juice
2 tsp. vanilla
1 cup chopped nuts
3 cups sifted flour
1 tsp. salt
1 tsp. soda
1 tsp. baking powder
1 Tbsp. cinnamon

MAKES 2 LOAVES

In large mixing bowl, beat eggs, oil, and sugar. Stir in carrots, pineapple with juice, vanilla and nuts. Sift together flour, salt, soda, baking powder and cinnamon. Mix with carrot mixture thoroughly. Pour into two greased loaf pans and bake at 350° about 45 minutes or until done. Can also be baked in a 10 inch tube pan at 350° for 1 hour or until done.

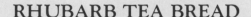

RHUBARB TEA BREAD

3 eggs
1 cup oil
2 cups brown sugar
2 tsp. vanilla
2½ cups rhubarb, chopped
½ cup walnuts, chopped
3 cups flour
2 tsp. soda
2 tsp. cinnamon
1 tsp. salt
½ tsp. baking powder
½ tsp. nutmeg
½ tsp. allspice

MAKES 2 LOAVES
Beat eggs until thick and foamy. Add oil, brown sugar, and vanilla. Beat well. Stir in rhubarb and walnuts. Add remaining ingredients and mix well. Turn into two greased and floured loaf pans. Bake 1 hour at 350°.

ZUCCHINI BREAD

3 eggs, well beaten
2 cups sugar
3 tsp. vanilla
1 cup oil
2 cups shredded zucchini
  (unpeeled)
3 cups flour
½ tsp. baking powder
1 tsp. salt
1 tsp. soda
1 tsp. cinnamon
½ cup nuts, chopped
1 cup coconut, optional
1 cup chocolate chips,
  optional

MAKES 2 LOAVES
Beat eggs until light and fluffy. Add sugar, vanilla, and oil. Blend well. Stir in zucchini. Sift together flour, baking powder, salt, soda and cinnamon. Blend with egg mixture. Fold in nuts and coconut and chocolate chips if desired. Turn into two greased and floured 9 x 5 inch loaf pans. Bake at 350° for 1 hour.

BREAD

EASY BUBBLE BREAD

4 tubes buttermilk
  biscuits
¾ cup sugar
1 Tbsp. cinnamon
½ cup pecans, chopped
1 cup sugar
1 cup pancake syrup
1½ sticks butter

SERVES 8
Cut each biscuit into fourths and roll in mixture of cinnamon and ¾ cup sugar. Grease tube pan. Arrange biscuit pieces in layers, topping each layer with pecans. Sprinkle cinnamon-sugar mixture over top layer, using no more than ½ cup. Let sit 45 minutes before baking (or overnight). Melt together sugar, syrup and butter. Bring to boil and boil 1 minute. Pour over bread and bake at 350° for 1 hour. Turn onto serving dish which should have a lip to catch extra syrup which may run off as it cools.

GRANDMA WHITE'S PURPLE PLUM BUCKLE

½ cup margarine
¾ cup sugar
1 egg
1¾ cup flour
1¾ tsp. baking powder
¼ tsp. salt
½ cup + 1 Tbsp. milk
1 Tbsp. cinnamon
  topping
10-12 purple plums, sliced

CINNAMON TOPPING:
½ cup flour
½ cup sugar
½ tsp. cinnamon
½ stick butter

Combine topping ingredients in bowl and mix until crumbly. Cream ½ cup margarine and sugar, add egg and beat until fluffy. Add dry ingredients and 1 tablespoon of the topping alternately with milk. Pour batter in a 9 x 9 inch greased dish. Arrange the sliced plums on top. Sprinkle topping over plums. Bake 40-45 minutes at 375° or until golden brown. Serve as a coffee cake, or top with ice cream or whipped cream for dessert.

ORANGE COFFEE CAKE

1 pkg. yeast
½ cup warm water
1 pkg. white cake mix
¼ cup orange juice
2 eggs

STREUSEL TOPPING:
½ cup flour
1 cup brown sugar (packed)
1 Tbsp. cinnamon
¼ cup butter, softened

GLAZE:
1 cup powdered sugar
2 Tbsp. butter, softened
2-3 Tbsp. orange juice

Dissolve yeast in warm water. Blend with cake mix, orange juice, and eggs. Beat well. Spread half the batter (about 2 cups) into a 9 x 13 inch pan. Sprinkle half the streusel topping over batter. Repeat with remaining batter and topping. Bake at 375° for 25-30 minutes. Drizzle glaze over warm cake.

CHOCOLATE CHIP COFFEE RING

1 cup sugar
½ cup butter or margarine
2 cups flour
1 cup sour cream
2 eggs
1 tsp. double-action
   baking powder
1¼ tsp. soda
1 tsp. vanilla
½ cup chocolate chips

TOPPING:
½ cup flour
½ cup packed light brown
   sugar
1½ tsp. cocoa
¼ cup butter
½ cup walnuts or pecans,
   chopped
1½ cup chocolate chips

Preheat oven to 350°. Grease 9 inch tube or Bundt pan. Beat sugar with ½ cup butter until light and fluffy. Add 2 cups flour and next five ingredients; beat at low speed until blended, constantly scraping bowl with rubber spatula. Increase speed to medium; beat 3 minutes. Stir in ½ cup chocolate chips. Spread batter evenly in pan.

In another bowl, measure ½ cup flour, brown sugar and cocoa. With pastry blender, cut in ¼ cup butter until the mixture resembles coarse crumbs. Stir in nuts and chocolate chips. Crumble mixture evenly over batter. Bake 60-65 minutes until cake pulls away from sides of pan. Cool completely. With small spatula, loosen cake from pan and remove.

BREAD

GRANDMA EATON'S COFFEE CAKE

2 cups flour
2 tsp. baking powder
1 tsp. salt
¾ cup sugar
2 rounded Tbsp. Crisco
1 cup milk

TOPPING:
2 Tbsp. melted butter
½ tsp. cinnamon
3 Tbsp. brown sugar

In mixing bowl, combine flour, baking powder, salt, sugar and Crisco. Set aside ¾ cup mixture for topping. Add milk to remainder of flour mixture, and mix until smooth. Pour batter into 8 x 8 inch buttered pan, and crumble topping over it. Bake at 350° for 30 minutes.

Topping: Combine melted butter, cinnamon, brown sugar, and ¾ cup of flour mixture; mix well.

SWEDISH PANCAKES

PANCAKE BATTER:
3 eggs
1¼ cup milk
¾ cup flour
1 Tbsp. sugar
½ tsp. salt

BERRY FILLING:
1 cup berries (strawberries or blueberries)
1/8 cup cold water
1 Tbsp. cornstarch
Sugar to taste (1/8-¼ cup)

MAKES 15
Combine batter ingredients in bowl and beat with mixer until smooth. Butter a round teflon skillet. Over medium heat, pour a thin (1/8 inch) layer of batter in bottom of pan. Cook as if making crepes. Cook on both sides for about a minute, or until firm and golden brown. Fill with thickened berry mixture, roll up, and top with powdered sugar and whipped cream.

To make berry mixture, put berries and water in a small saucepan. Add sugar and cornstarch which has been dissolved in 1/8 cup water. Stir over medium heat until thickened. These are a special treat on Sunday morning or for breakfast guests.

NEW ORLEANS DOUGHNUTS (BEIGNETS)

1 pkg. active dry yeast
1½ cups warm water
  (105°)
½ cup sugar
1 tsp. salt
2 eggs
1 cup undiluted evaporated
  milk
7 cups flour
¼ cup soft shortening
Oil for frying
Powdered sugar or honey

MAKES 4 DOZEN
In large bowl, sprinkle yeast over water; stir to dissolve. Add sugar, salt, eggs, and milk. Blend with beater. Add 4 cups of flour; beat until smooth. Add shortening; beat in remaining flour. Cover and chill several hours. Dough will keep in refrigerator 4-5 days. Roll on floured board to 1/8 inch thickness. Cut into 2½ inch squares. Deep fry at 360° 2-3 minutes or until lightly browned on both sides. Drain on paper towel. Sprinkle heavily with powdered sugar. Also good with butter or honey. Serve hot at breakfast or brunch.

SOPAPILLAS

1 pkg. yeast
¼ cup water
1½ cups milk
3 Tbsp. shortening, melted
1½ tsp. salt
2 Tbsp. sugar
5 cups flour

MAKES 3 DOZEN
Mix all ingredients and knead briefly. Let rest one hour. Roll very thin, cut into triangles and fry in deep fat until brown on both sides. Dough can be kept for 2 days in refrigerator. Drizzle with honey and serve warm. They will add the perfect finishing touch to your Mexican food dinner.

BREAD

APPLE MUFFINS

1 cup sugar
½ cup margarine, softened
1 cup milk
1 egg
1½ cup flour
1/8 tsp. salt
2 tsp. baking powder
½ tsp. cinnamon
1 tsp. lemon juice
1 cup apples, grated

MAKES ABOUT 20 MUFFINS
Cream sugar and margarine. Add rest of ingredients in order given, being careful not to stir too much. Fill greased or lined muffin tins ⅔ full and bake at 425° for 20-25 minutes.

BLUEBERRY MUFFINS

⅔ cup shortening
1 cup sugar
3 eggs
3 cups flour
2 heaping tsp. baking powder
1 tsp. salt
1 cup milk
1 can blueberries, drained well

MAKES 2 DOZEN MUFFINS
Cream shortening and sugar. Add three eggs, one at a time, beating after each. Sift dry ingredients and add alternately with the 1 cup milk. Fold in 1 can drained blueberries. Fill greased muffin cups ⅔ full and bake at 375° until browned, about 20 minutes. This mixture will keep in the refrigerator 2-3 weeks.

CINNAMON-SUGAR MUFFINS

1½ cups flour
¾ cup sugar
2 tsp. baking powder
¼ tsp. salt
¼ tsp. nutmeg
½ cup milk
1 egg, beaten
⅓ cup butter, melted
1 tsp. cinnamon
½ cup sugar
½ tsp. vanilla
⅓ cup butter, melted

MAKES 2 DOZEN MUFFINS
Mix flour, sugar, baking powder, salt, and nutmeg. Add milk, beaten egg, and ⅓ cup melted butter. Mix well. Fill greased or lined muffin tins ⅔ full and bake at 400° for 20 minutes. Remove while still hot, dip in melted butter, then mixture of sugar, cinnamon and vanilla.

OATMEAL MUFFINS

1 cup quick oats
1 cup buttermilk
1 egg
½ cup brown sugar,
   packed
½ cup vegetable oil
1 cup flour
1 tsp. baking powder
½ tsp. salt
½ tsp. baking soda

MAKES 1 DOZEN MUFFINS
Mix all ingredients and spoon batter into greased muffin tins ⅔ full. Bake at 400° for 15-20 minutes.

ORANGE MUFFINS

1 cup butter or margarine
1 cup sugar
2 eggs
1 tsp. soda
1 cup buttermilk
2 cups sifted flour
2 Tbsp. grated orange rind
Juice of 2 oranges
1 cup brown sugar

MAKES 18-24 MUFFINS
Cream butter and sugar. Add eggs and beat well. Stir soda into buttermilk, and add alternately with flour to batter mixture. Stir in rind. Fill lined or greased muffin tins ⅔ full and bake at 400° for 20-25 minutes. Mix orange juice with brown sugar. Pour over hot muffins that have been poked with fork. Remove from pan immediately.

BREAD

ORANGE HONEY SURPRISE MUFFINS

1 orange, cut into thin
   pieces (peeling, too)
12 Tbsp. honey
1 egg
½ cup milk
¼ cup salad oil
1½ cups flour
½ cup sugar
2 tsp. baking powder
½ tsp. salt

MAKES 1 DOZEN
Heat oven to 400°. Grease 12 muffin cups. Put several pieces of orange and one tablespoon of honey in bottom of each cup. Beat egg; stir in milk and oil. Combine dry ingredients in bowl, mix well and add to milk mixture. Stir ingredients just until flour is moistened. Batter will be lumpy. Fill muffin cups ⅔ full. Bake 20-25 minutes or until golden brown. Serve orange slices up. Serve at brunch or luncheon.

PINEAPPLE MUFFINS

1—9 oz. can undrained
   crushed pineapple
1 cup oatmeal
½ cup sour cream
⅓ cup shortening
⅓ cup brown sugar
1 tsp. grated orange rind
1 egg, beaten
1¼ cup flour
1 tsp. baking powder
½ tsp. soda
1 tsp. salt

MAKES 1 DOZEN
Combine pineapple, oatmeal and sour cream. Let stand 15 minutes. Cream shortening, brown sugar and orange rind. Add beaten egg. Sift together flour, baking powder, soda and salt. Add flour mixture alternately with the pineapple mixture to batter. Fill greased muffin cups ⅔ full. Bake for 25 minutes at 400°.

BREAD

RAISIN BRAN MUFFINS

15 oz. Raisin Bran
5 cups flour
3 cups sugar
5 tsp. soda
2 tsp. salt
1 cup oil
1 quart buttermilk
4 eggs, beaten

MAKES 5 DOZEN
Combine dry ingredients in a LARGE mixing bowl. Stir until all ingredients are well mixed. Add oil, buttermilk and eggs. Mix until all ingredients are moist. Spoon into greased or lined muffin tin, filling cups ⅔ full. Bake at 400° for 15-20 minutes. This batter keeps well in the refrigerator for two weeks, and makes outstanding muffins!

ONE MINUTE DOUGHNUTS

Tube of refrigerator
  biscuits
Oil for cooking
Chocolate frosting or sugar

Heat oil to 375°. Poke hole in center of biscuit. Deep fry to a golden brown on both sides. Roll in sugar or frost. Quick and easy treat for kids or breakfast.

BREAD

BAKING POWDER BISCUITS

3 cups flour
2 Tbsp. baking powder
1½ tsp. salt
1 cup vegetable shortening
1 cup milk
3 Tbsp. butter, melted
(optional)

MAKES 16-20 BISCUITS
Sift flour, baking powder, and salt together in large bowl. Add shortening and cut into dry ingredients with pastry blender, until it resembles coarse meal. Make a well in the center of mixture and pour in milk. Mix together only long enough to form a soft dough. Knead it for about 30 seconds and roll dough about ½ inch thick. Cut the dough into 2 inch rounds with cookie cutter or water glass. Gather together any remaining dough, roll again, and cut more. Brush with butter if you desire. Arrange biscuits on a cookie sheet, and bake in the middle of oven at 400° for 20 minutes.

EASY BREAKFAST CINNAMON BREAD

1 stick butter or margarine,
melted
½ cup brown sugar,
packed
½ cup finely chopped nuts
1 pkg. Rhodes frozen
dinner rolls
Cinnamon

Grease tube pan well. Pour half the melted butter into pan and sprinkle with brown sugar, cinnamon, and most of the nuts. Put the frozen rolls on top of this, packing them in. Sprinkle with remaining nuts and more cinnamon. Pour remaining half of melted butter over rolls. Cover and let sit out overnight. In the morning, bake in 375° oven for 20-30 minutes. Turn upside down on plate to let topping run down. Serve warm. This is a very easy and delicious way to have hot cinnamon rolls for breakfast.

BUTTERSCOTCH ROLLS

1 pkg. butterscotch
   pudding mix
1½ cups milk
1 pkg. yeast
¼ cup warm water
2 eggs, beaten
1 stick oleo, melted
2 tsp. salt
4-4½ cups flour

FILLING:
¼ cup butter, melted
⅔ cup brown sugar
⅔ cup coconut
⅔ cup pecans, chopped
2 Tbsp. flour

FROSTING:
2 Tbsp. butter
2 Tbsp. milk
¼ cup brown sugar
1 cup powdered sugar

MAKES 2 DOZEN
Combine butterscotch pudding and milk in small saucepan. Cook until pudding boils. Let cool. Dissolve yeast in ¼ cup warm water. Combine yeast mixture, cooled pudding, eggs, oleo, salt and 2 cups of the flour in bowl. Beat well. Add enough remaining flour to make a soft dough. Turn onto floured board, knead well, and roll out ¼ inch thick. Combine melted butter, brown sugar, coconut, pecans, and flour in bowl. Spread this filling over dough. Roll up jelly roll style and cut into 1 inch rolls. Place in greased pan. Let rise until double. Bake 25-30 minutes at 375°. Blend together frosting ingredients and frost slightly warm rolls.

ORANGE ROLLS

2 pkg. dry yeast
1 cup lukewarm water
1 tsp. salt
⅓ cup sugar
⅓ cup salad oil
2 eggs, well beaten
4 cups flour

ORANGE BUTTER:
¼ cup frozen orange juice,
   undiluted
1⅓ sticks butter
1 box powdered sugar

MAKES 2 DOZEN
Dissolve the yeast in 1 cup lukewarm water. Add salt, sugar, oil and eggs; beat well. Add flour, 2 cups at a time, beating after each addition. Knead well, place in bowl and cover with damp tea towel. Let rise until more than doubled in bulk. Make into rolls (try cloverleaf style . . . roll the dough into 1 inch balls and drop three at a time in a greased muffin tin.) Let rise again and bake at 375° for 20-25 minutes. Spread warm rolls with orange butter. These are a memorable dinner roll.

BREAD

CREAM CHEESE SWEET ROLLS

1 pkg. dry yeast
¼ cup warm water
¾ cup buttermilk
1 egg
2¾ to 3 cups all purpose
　flour
¼ cup butter
¼ cup sugar
1 tsp. baking powder
1 tsp. salt

FILLING:
1—8 oz. pkg. cream
　cheese, softened
½ cup sugar
3 Tbsp. flour
1 egg yolk

Chopped nuts
Strawberry, cherry or
　blueberry preserves
Powdered sugar glaze

MAKES 2-3 DOZEN
Dissolve yeast in warm water. Add buttermilk, egg, 1 cup flour, butter, sugar, baking powder and salt. Mix well for 2 minutes. Stir in enough remaining flour to make soft dough.

Roll dough very thin, 1/8 inch thick, and cut into 3 inch squares. Combine filling ingredients and mix well. Place dough square onto greased baking sheets. Place 1 heaping tablespoon filling in center of each square. Bring two diagonally opposite corners to center of each square and pinch together to seal. Bake 12-15 minutes at 375°. If you desire, top each square with a spoonful of preserves or powdered sugar glaze. Sprinkle with nuts. These will absolutely melt in your mouth!

BEER BREAD

3 cups self-rising flour
¼ cup sugar
1 can beer

MAKES 1 LOAF
Pour sugar in bowl. Add beer and stir well. Gradually stir in flour. When well blended, pour into greased loaf pan. Bake at 350° for 1 hour. Great at dinner time but even better for toast the next morning! This is a quick bread that is easy for anyone to make.

EILEEN'S MONKEY BREAD

2 pkg. dry yeast
1 cup lukewarm water
1 cup shortening
¾ cup sugar
1½ tsp. salt
1 cup boiling water
2 eggs, beaten
6 cups flour
1 stick butter, melted

MAKES 2 PANS
Dissolve yeast in warm water. Mix together shortening, sugar, and salt; add boiling water and mix well. Add eggs and stir. Add flour and dissolved yeast to shortening mixture, alternately, until well blended. Knead well. Let rise until double in bulk. Roll to ¼ to ½ inch thickness. Cut in various shapes and sizes. Dip in melted butter and place in tube pans until half full; let rise until doubled. Bake at 350° for 35-45 minutes or until brown. After mixing and rising once, dough may be punched down and refrigerated to be used later. Be sure to cover with damp cloth. Note: Use a tube pan, or a small pan. If put in regular loaf pans, the dough does not get cooked in the middle. This makes a delicious easy bread for your family.

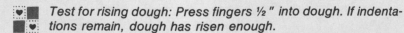
Test for rising dough: Press fingers ½" into dough. If indentations remain, dough has risen enough.

BREAD

MAMA LANG'S CINNAMON ROLLS OR WHITE BREAD

½ cup shortening
½ cup sugar
2 cups boiling water
2 tsp. salt
3 cups flour
2 eggs
2 pkg. yeast
½ cup lukewarm water
4 cups flour

CINNAMON ROLL FILLING:
½ cup softened butter or margarine
¾-1 cup brown sugar
2½ tsp. cinnamon
¾ cup walnuts or pecans, chopped (optional)
¾ cup raisins (optional)

FROSTING:
2 Tbsp. butter, softened
6-7 Tbsp. milk
1 tsp. vanilla
2 cups powdered sugar

MAKES 4 DOZEN ROLLS, OR 2 LOAVES

Put shortening and sugar in large bowl, cover with boiling water. Let cool. Add salt and 3 cups flour, one at a time. Beat well. Add 2 eggs, then yeast dissolved in water. Stir well. Add 4 cups flour, beating after each cup. Knead well on a floured board. Place in bowl and cover with damp tea towel. Let rise until doubled in bulk; punch down. Put dough in refrigerator, cover with wet cloth and plate, and let sit overnight.

To roll dough for cinnamon rolls, divide in half, and roll to ¼ inch thickness. Spread the dough with softened butter, sprinkle with brown sugar, then cinnamon, raisins and nuts if you choose, and roll in a jelly roll fashion. Seal the edges by pinching them together. Cut into 1 inch rolls and place in a greased muffin tin or pan. Let rise until doubled. Bake at 375° for 10-15 minutes. When cooled, ice with mixture of butter, milk, vanilla and powdered sugar.

To make loaves of bread, divide the dough in half, after it has risen once, roll out, shape into loaves, put in greased loaf pans, cover with damp tea towel and let rise again. Bake at 350° for 20-30 minutes, or until golden brown and hollow-sounding when tapped. Brush with melted butter and immediately set on racks to cool.

64

WHOLE WHEAT BREAD

6 Tbsp. Crisco, melted
¾ cup scalded milk
4 Tbsp. sugar
3½ tsp. salt
3/8 cup molasses
1½ cup warm water
2 pkg. dry yeast
4½ cups whole wheat flour
2 cups sifted white flour

MAKES 2 LOAVES

Melt shortening, add milk, sugar, salt and molasses. Cool to lukewarm. Dissolve yeast in warm water. Stir milk and molasses mixture into yeast mixture. Add 2 cups whole wheat flour. Beat until bubbly. Stir in remaining flour. Knead well. Place in large bowl and cover with damp tea towel. Let rise until doubled. Punch down, let rise again. Divide into 2 equal parts, and roll out for loaves. Place in greased loaf pans, let rise until doubled. Bake at 375° for 10 minutes, lower the temperature to 350° and bake 20 more minutes. Bread is done when it sounds hollow when tapped. Brush melted butter on top, take out of pans, and cool on wire racks. This whole wheat bread is light and a little sweet, unlike most whole wheat breads. It is a real winner! For something different, try baking one half of this bread in a greased 2 lb. coffee can.

 To form loaves for bread; roll dough into rectangle, 18 x 9 inches. Roll up from short side. Pinch ends and bottom seam to seal and fold ends under. Place seam side down in greased pan. Bake loaves with the top of pan in the middle of the oven.

BREAD

■●■●♥●■●■●♥●■●♥●■●■●♥●■●♥●■●■●♥●■●♥●■●■●♥●■●♥

SOURDOUGH BREAD AND STARTER

STARTER:
1 pkg. dry yeast
2 cups warm water
2 cups flour

SOURDOUGH BREAD:
1 pkg. dry yeast
¼ cup warm water
1 tsp. sugar
1 egg
¼ cup vegetable oil
½ cup water
1 tsp. salt
⅓ cup sugar
1 cup sourdough starter
3½ cups flour
Cornmeal
Melted butter

3 CUPS STARTER AND 2 LOAVES

Combine starter ingredients in large bowl (not metal). Mix well and let stand, covered loosely with plastic wrap, at room temperature for 48 hours. To store starter, refrigerate in a jar with a loose-fitting lid. When making bread, stir starter well, pour out required amount and replenish starter with 1 cup flour, 1 cup milk, ⅓ cup sugar. Replenish at least once a week.

Dissolve yeast in water, stir in sugar. Let sit 15 minutes. Mix egg, oil, water, salt, and sugar in large mixing bowl (not metal). Add starter and yeast mixture. Stir well. Blend in 2 cups flour and beat well. Add remainder of flour. Knead well, adding more flour if dough seems sticky. Place dough in a bowl, cover with a damp tea towel and let rise until doubled. Punch down, and knead again for 2-3 minutes. Shape dough, place on greased baking sheets that have been sprinkled with cornmeal; brush with butter. Cover and let rise until doubled. Bake at 350° for about 20-25 minutes. Brush with butter after baking if desired. Once you get in the habit of making this bread, no meal will be complete without it.

 When bread is baking, a small dish of water in the oven will help to keep the crust from getting hard.

CRACKED WHEAT BREAD

½ cup cracked wheat
(bulgar)
2 cups warm water
1 pkg. dry yeast
¼ cup brown sugar
¼ cup white sugar
(scant ¼ cup)
2 tsp. salt
1 Tbsp. vegetable oil
About 5 cups flour

MAKES 2 LOAVES

Soak bulgar in 1 cup warm water 15 minutes. Dissolve yeast in the other cup of water. Add to bulgar. Add sugar, salt, and oil. Mix well. Add flour, a cup at a time, stirring well after each addition. Add flour until a soft dough forms. Let dough rest 10 minutes. Turn out on a floured board and knead well. Place in bowl, cover with damp tea towel, and let rise until doubled. Punch down, let rise again. Cut in half, roll out and place in 2 greased loaf pans. Let rise again. Bake at 375° for 20-25 minutes.

BAR L ROLLS

3 heaping Tbsp. Crisco
1 Tbsp. salt
Scant ½ cup sugar
1 cup hot water
6 cups flour
1 cup lukewarm water
2 pkg. yeast

MAKES 3 DOZEN

Combine Crisco, salt, and sugar in large bowl. Pour 1 cup hot water over mixture and stir until Crisco melts. Add enough flour to make a paste (about 1 cup). Add 1 cup lukewarm water, in which yeast has been dissolved. Mix in remaining flour to form a soft dough. Knead dough well. Place in bowl and cover with damp tea towel; let rise. Punch down when doubled and roll to ½-¾ inch thickness. Cut with cookie cutter and place on greased pans about ½ inch apart. Let rise until doubled. Bake at 400° for 20 minutes or until brown. This was Grandmother's recipe, one she did by look and feel. This written out version produces light and tasty rolls, as close to hers as possible!

BREAD

BRAIDED POTATO BREAD

1 pkg. dry yeast
   dissolved in ¼ cup
   warm water
3½ cups flour
¼ cup sugar
1½ tsp. salt
1 cup mashed potatoes
⅔ cup milk
¼ cup butter or margarine,
   melted
2 eggs
1 tsp. water
1 egg white
2 tsp. poppy seeds

MAKES 1 LOAF

Mix 1½ cups flour, the sugar, and salt in a large mixing bowl. In separate bowl, combine potatoes, milk, butter and eggs, and yeast mixture. Add to flour mixture. Beat 2 minutes on medium speed, scraping bowl occasionally. Stir in enough remaining flour to handle. Knead dough on a well-floured board until smooth and elastic. Place in bowl and let rise in warm place until double in bulk. Punch down and divide the dough into thirds. Shape each third into a roll, 14 inches long. Braid rolls on greased baking sheet, being careful not to stretch dough. Fold ends under loaf. Let rise until almost double. Heat oven to 350°. Beat egg white and water slightly, brush on bread. Sprinkle with poppy seed. Bake until golden brown, about 30-35 minutes. Cool on a wire rack.

CROISSANTS

2 pkg. dry yeast
1 cup warm water
5 cups unsifted flour
¾ cup evaporated milk
1½ tsp. salt
1 egg
⅓ cup sugar
¼ cup butter, melted
1 cup chilled butter
1 egg, beaten with 1
  Tbsp. water

MAKES 3 DOZEN

Sprinkle yeast over warm water in large bowl. Add 1 cup flour, evaporated milk, salt, egg, sugar and melted butter. Beat until smooth. In separate bowl, cut chilled butter into remaining flour until butter particles are the size of peas. Pour yeast batter over the top. Fold in until all flour is moist. Cover bowl with plastic wrap. Chill 4 hours. Can be refrigerated several days. Handle dough as little as possible. Divide in half, keeping other half cool until ready to work. Knead 6-7 times and roll ¼ of the dough into a ¼ inch thick circle on floured board. Cut dough circle into pie shaped wedges. Roll each loosely towards point. Place on ungreased cookie sheet. Cover lightly. Let rise until double. (Don't speed rising by placing them in a warm spot.) When doubled, brush with egg and water mixture. Bake in preheated 400° oven for 12-15 minutes.

BREAD

TEXAS BUTTERMILK BISCUITS

5 cups unbleached flour
3 Tbsp. sugar
1 Tbsp. baking powder
1 tsp. salt
1 cup butter or margarine
2 envelopes dry yeast
¼ cup warm water
2 cups buttermilk
¾ cup butter or margarine, melted

MAKES 3-4 DOZEN
Sift together dry ingredients into a large bowl. Using knife or pastry blender, cut butter into dry mixture until it is like coarse meal. Dissolve yeast in warm water and add to mixture. Add buttermilk and blend thoroughly. Roll or pat into ¼ inch thickness. Cut with cookie cutter or water glass. Dip each biscuit in melted butter, then fold in half and press edges together. Place on a baking sheet and freeze until firm. Package in plastic bags and freeze. May be baked without defrosting at 350° about 15-20 minutes or until golden brown. A versatile, richly-flavored biscuit... good at breakfast or dinner.

HOMESTYLE CORN BREAD

1 cup yellow cornmeal
1 cup flour
¼ cup sugar
4 tsp. baking powder
½ tsp. salt.
1 cup milk
1 egg
¼ cup vegetable oil

MAKES 1 DOZEN MUFFINS, 14 CORN STICKS OR 1 8-INCH SQUARE PAN
Mix cornmeal, flour, sugar, baking powder and salt. Add milk, egg and shortening and beat until smooth. Pour into greased or lined muffin tins, or corn stick pans and bake at 425° 15-20 minutes. It can also be baked in a greased 8-inch square pan at 425° for 20-25 minutes.

MEXICAN CORN BREAD

1 cup yellow cornmeal
1½ tsp. salt
1 Tbsp. baking powder
2 eggs, beaten
1—8 oz. can cream-style
  corn
⅔ cup corn oil
1—8 oz. carton sour cream
1—4 oz. can green chiles,
  chopped and drained
1 tsp. sugar
2 cups Longhorn cheese,
  grated

SERVES 9
Mix together cornmeal, salt and baking powder; add eggs, corn, oil, and sour cream. Mix well and pour half of the batter into an 8-inch square, greased baking pan. Spread green chiles, 1 cup cheese, and sugar over this. Cover with remaining half of batter. Top with one cup of cheese. Bake 1 hour at 350°.

HUSH PUPPIES

1 cup cornmeal
1 tsp. baking powder
1 tsp. salt
1 tsp. sugar
1 cup flour
1 egg, beaten
¾ cup milk
Dash of Tabasco
1 Tbsp. grated onion

MAKES ABOUT 24
Sift dry ingredients into a bowl. Add beaten egg and milk to cornmeal mixture. Mix in onion and Tabasco. Drop by heaping teaspoons into hot fat (375°) and fry until brown. Drain and serve with a fish fry dinner.

BREAD

BEST IRISH SODA BREAD

4½ cups all purpose flour
4 tsp. baking powder
½ tsp. baking soda
1 tsp. salt
3 Tbsp. sugar
1 Tbsp. caraway seeds
1 cup seedless raisins
2 cups buttermilk
Butter
Powdered sugar

Heat oven to 350°. Grease and flour a 9 inch cast iron skillet. (A round cake pan works well also.) Mix 4 cups of flour with baking powder, soda, salt, sugar and caraway seeds. Stir in raisins, making sure they are separated. Add buttermilk all at once and mix with a fork to form a dough. Sprinkle about ¼ cup of remaining flour on a work surface, turn out dough and knead for about 5 minutes until smooth. Use only as much of remaining ¼ cup flour as needed to prevent dough from sticking. Form dough into a smooth, round loaf and press into pan. With a sharp knife, cut a cross ½ inch deep, across top of dough. Bake for one hour or until loaf is lightly browned and sounds hollow when tapped. Remove bread to wire rack, rub top with butter and dust with powdered sugar. Good with extra butter and powdered sugar on each slice.

ONION BREAD

Frozen bread dough or your
    favorite white bread
    dough
1 pkg. onion soup mix
1 cup melted butter

Form dough into small balls. Combine onion soup mixture with melted butter. Roll each ball in butter mixture, and arrange in buttered tube pan. Let double and bake at 375° for 45 minutes. Turn cooked bread onto serving plate. Pass remaining butter/onion mixture with bread. Dip each piece into butter mixture before eating.

KATHI'S DILLY BREAD

1 pkg. yeast
¼ cup warm water
1 cup cottage cheese
2 Tbsp. sugar
1 Tbsp. minced onion
1 Tbsp. butter
2 tsp. dill seed
1 tsp. salt
¼ tsp. soda
1 unbeaten egg
2¼-2½ cups flour

Dissolve yeast in water. In bowl combine cottage cheese, sugar, onion, butter, dill seed, salt, soda, egg and softened yeast. Add flour to form stiff dough; beat well after each addition. Cover. Let rise in warm place until light and double in size, 50-60 minutes. Stir down dough. Turn into well greased 8 inch round casserole. Let rise in warm place about 30-40 minutes. Bake at 350° for 40-50 minutes or until golden brown. Brush with butter and sprinkle with dill seed. For a hearty winter lunoh, oorvo thio with Homomade Vegetable Soup and a green salad.

Salads

RED, WHITE AND BLUEBERRY SALAD

1—3 oz. pkg. raspberry
   gelatin
2 cups water
1 envelope unflavored
   gelatin
½ cup cold water
1 cup half and half
½ cup sugar
1—8 oz. pkg. cream
   cheese, softened
½ cup walnuts, chopped
1 tsp. vanilla
1½ cups frozen blueberries
   (may substitute 1 can
   blueberries)
1—3 oz. pkg. black
   raspberry gelatin
2 cups water

SERVES 10-12

Dissolve raspberry gelatin in 1 cup boiling water. Add 1 cup cold water. Pour into 13 x 9 inch pan or large ring mold. Refrigerate to firm, but not set. Add unflavored gelatin to ½ cup cold water, stir to let soften. Combine half and half, and sugar in small saucepan. Cook over low heat but do not boil. Add unflavored gelatin and let mixture get very warm, but do not boil. Pour into bowl with softened cream cheese and beat with mixer. Add chopped nuts and vanilla. Cool to room temperature. Spoon over raspberry layer. Chill until firm. Dissolve package of black raspberry gelatin in one cup boiling water. Add one cup of cold water and blueberries. (If using canned blueberries, omit the last cup of cold water and pour in the blueberries undrained.) Chill until thick, then pour over cream cheese layer. Chill until firm. This large salad is great for family get-togethers.

BANANA-BERRY GELATIN SALAD

1—3 oz. pkg. strawberry
   gelatin
2 cups water
1—10 oz. pkg. frozen
   strawberries
2 bananas, mashed
1 cup whipped cream

SERVES 4-6

Dissolve gelatin in 1 cup hot water; add frozen strawberries. Add mashed bananas and a cup of cold water. Mix well. Pour into 8 x 8 inch pan or mold. Chill until firm. Spread whipped cream over top. Refrigerate. (A can of crushed pineapple is also good in this salad. Use a large box of gelatin and omit the second cup of water.)

■♥■♥■♥■♥■♥■♥■♥■♥■♥■♥■♥■♥■♥■

DIVINE RASPBERRY SALAD

**Juice from crushed
   pineapple plus water to
   make 1 cup
1—3 oz. pkg. lemon gelatin
1½ cups miniature or diced
   marshmallows
1—8 oz. pkg. cream cheese
½ pint whipping cream
2 Tbsp. sugar
¼ tsp. vanilla
1 can crushed pineapple,
   (2½ cups)
2 cups water
2—3 oz. pkg. raspberry
   gelatin
1 lb. pkg. frozen
   raspberries, thawed**

SERVES 10-12
Dissolve lemon gelatin in boiling pine-apple juice and water. Pour over marshmallows and cream cheese. Beat with mixer. Whip cream, add sugar and vanilla. Add to gelatin mix-ture. Fold in crushed pineapple, and pour into 9 x 13 inch pan. Allow to set. Dissolve raspberry gelatin in two cups boiling water. Add berries; cool. Spoon over first layer. Refrigerate and let set.

LIME-PEAR GELATIN SALAD

**1—3 oz. pkg. lime gelatin
1½ cups water
1—16 oz. can pears, sliced
1—3 oz. pkg. lemon gelatin
1 cup water
1—3 oz. pkg. cream cheese
½ cup water
1 cup cream, whipped**

SERVES 8
Dissolve lime gelatin in one cup boiling water. Add ½ cup cold water and undrained pears. Pears may be sliced more if desired. Pour into 8 x 8 inch pan. Refrigerate until firm. Dis-solve lemon gelatin in one cup boiling water. Pour over cream cheese and beat with mixer. Mix in ½ cup cold water. Fold in whipped cream. Pour over lime gelatin layer and chill to set.

SALADS

PEACHES 'N CREAM SALAD

2—3 oz. pkg. lemon gelatin
2 cups boiling water
1—3 oz. pkg. cream cheese
1 cup whipping cream
2 Tbsp. sugar
1 cup orange juice
½ cup pecans, chopped
1—1 lb. 6 oz. can peach
   pie filling

SERVES 10-12
Dissolve one package lemon gelatin in one cup boiling water. Pour into bowl with cream cheese. Beat with mixer. Whip cream; sweeten with 2 tablespoons sugar. Add orange juice and whipped cream to cream cheese mixture. Beat with mixer. Add pecans. Pour into 9 x 13 inch pan or mold. Chill until firm. Dissolve second box of gelatin in one cup boiling water. Add the peach pie filling. Let cool. Pour over first layer and chill until firm.

BLUEBERRY SALAD

2—3 oz. pkg. blackberry
   gelatin (or black cherry
   gelatin)
2 cups water
1 small can crushed
   pineapple, drained; save
   juice
2 cups blueberries

TOPPING:
1 carton sour cream (small)
2—3 oz. pkg. cream cheese
½ cup sugar
½ tsp. vanilla

SERVES 10-12
Dissolve gelatin in 2 cups boiling water. Add pineapple juice and enough water to make another cup. Add pineapple and blueberries. Pour into 9 x 13 inch pan. Let set.

Blend topping ingredients and spread over blueberry gelatin mixture. Refrigerate.

 Spray the mold for a gelatin salad lightly with Pam before pouring it in. The jello salad will unmold with ease.

$1000 ORANGE SALAD

1—3 oz. pkg. orange
  gelatin
1 cup boiling water
1—8 oz. bottle 7-Up
½ pt. whipping cream
1 small can crushed
  pineapple, drained
1 small jar maraschino
  cherries, drained
2 bananas, sliced
½ cup nuts, chopped
½ cup coconut

SERVES 9-12
Dissolve gelatin in boiling water. Add 7-Up and refrigerate about 45 minutes or until slightly jelled. Whip cream until stiff. Fold whipped cream and remaining ingredients into jello mixture. Pour into 9 x 13 inch pan or mold. Refrigerate until firm.

BING CHERRY GELATIN SALAD

1—1 lb. 4 oz. can bing
  cherries, reserve juice
1—3 oz. pkg. cherry gelatin
1 cup boiling water
1 cup juice from cherries,
  plus water
¼ cup walnuts, chopped
1—3 oz. pkg. cream cheese

SERVES 4-6
Dissolve cherry gelatin in boiling water. Drain juice from cherries and add enough water to make one cup. Add to gelatin. Pour into ring mold. Chill until partially set. Mix cream cheese with walnuts. Roll into marble size balls. Drop cherries and cheese balls alternately into cherry jello. Let set. Also good served with whipped cream on top.

JENNY'S FRUITED COTTAGE CHEESE

To creamed cottage cheese, add pineapple tidbits, seeded red and green grapes, diced apple (with the skin), a few broken nutmeats, and lemon juice to taste. This is a quick and easy salad, perfect with most any meal.

SALADS

MIXED FRUIT SALAD AND DRESSINGS

Oranges, peeled and diced
Apples, diced
Bananas, sliced
Blueberries, whole
Grapes, green or purple
    seedless
Marshmallows, miniature
    or diced
Coconut, flaked
Pineapple, chunked
Walnuts, broken
Cherries, white or bing
Maraschino cherries, halved
Mandarin oranges
Pears, fresh, diced
Cantaloupe balls
Honeydew balls
Watermelon balls
Strawberries

These ingredients can be used in any combination and proportion to suit your family's taste. Serve a fruit salad plain, or with one of the following favorite dressings.

SOUR CREAM-POWDERED SUGAR DRESSING:
½ cup sour cream
2 Tbsp. powdered sugar

Blend and mix into fruit salad.

WHIPPED CREAM DRESSING:
1 cup whipping cream
3-4 Tbsp. sugar
½ tsp. vanilla

Beat the ingredients until the cream is stiff. Mix with fruit.

VANILLA ICE CREAM DRESSING:
1-2 cups vanilla ice cream, softened

Mix the softened ice cream with fruit. This is delicious and easy.

YOGURT-HONEY DRESSING:
1 small carton plain yogurt
3-4 Tbsp. honey

Mix and toss with fruit salad. Use flavored yogurts with special salads. Example: strawberry yogurt with strawberry fruit salad.

POPPY SEED DRESSING:
1¼ cups sugar
2 tsp. dry mustard
2 tsp. salt
⅔ cup vinegar
3 Tbsp. onion juice
2 cups salad oil (not olive oil)
3 Tbsp. poppy seeds

Mix sugar, mustard, salt, and vinegar. Add onion juice and stir it in thoroughly. Add oil slowly, beating constantly until thick. Use a blender, food processor, or mixer for this part. Add poppy seeds and beat until well blended. This dressing is exceptional on any fruit salad. Try it on slices of pink grapefruit and avocado on a bed of lettuce for the best taste treat of all.

FRUIT SALAD DRESSING:
3 egg yolks
2 Tbsp. sugar
Dash of salt
2 Tbsp. vinegar
2 Tbsp. pineapple syrup
1 Tbsp. butter
1 cup whipped cream

Cook egg yolks, sugar, salt, vinegar, pineapple syrup and butter in double boiler until thick, stirring constantly. Cool. Stir into fruit salad. Fold in whipped cream. Chill 24 hours.

CRANBERRY SALAD

1 cup ground, raw cranberries
1 cup sugar
1 small can light cherries (Royal Sweet Cherries), drained
1 small can Bing cherries, drained
½ cup walnuts, chopped
1 cup mandarin oranges, drained (can use cut up fresh orange)
1½ cup whipping cream, whipped and sweetened with 2 Tbsp. sugar
1 cup miniature marshmallows

SERVES 8
Combine cranberries and sugar. Refrigerate overnight. Drain off liquid. Mix in cherries, nuts and oranges. Fold in whipped cream and marshmallows. Pour in serving dish and refrigerate. This is a good holiday salad.

 Heating an orange a moment in the oven will make the inner white skin peel off perfectly.

SALADS

CINNAMON APPLES

½ cup sugar
½ cup water
½ cup cinnamon candies
5-6 apples (Jonathans are best), peeled, cored, and sliced

SERVES 4
Combine sugar, water, and cinnamon candies in saucepan. Heat to dissolve candies and sugar. Add apples. Simmer slowly, covered, for 30 minutes. Uncover and simmer for 1 more hour. Can also be cooked in casserole dish in the oven; leave lid on for ½ hour, then remove lid and bake until syrup thickens, about 1 hour. Syrup will thicken more as it cools. Serve as a cold condiment at lunch or supper. This is a good way to use overripe apples.

PISTACHIO SALAD

1 pkg. instant pistachio pudding
1—8 oz. container whipped topping
1—6½ oz. can crushed pineapple, drained
1 cup small marshmallows
Nuts, chopped (walnuts, pistachios or pecans)

SERVES 6
Make pistachio pudding according to package directions. Add other ingredients and mix. Pour into serving dish; garnish with nuts. Refrigerate. For a variation, try putting this in a graham cracker crust and serving it for dessert! It is delicious either way.

 Scrape the sides of a cucumber with a fork before slicing for a fancy look.

CUCUMBER-VINEGAR SALAD

3 medium cucumbers
¼ medium onion, sliced
  thin
½ cup white vinegar
¼ cup water
2-3 Tbsp. sugar
Pepper to taste
½ tsp. salt

SERVES 4-6
Peel cucumbers and slice thin. Add sliced onion. Stir together vinegar, water, sugar, salt, and pepper. Pour over slices. Cover and refrigerate at least three hours, 7-10 hours is better. This is wonderful to serve with hamburgers at a backyard, summertime picnic.

CUCUMBERS AND SOUR CREAM

3-4 cucumbers, sliced thin
1 tsp. salt
1 small onion, sliced thin
  (or 6 green onions,
  sliced)
1—8 oz. carton sour cream
3 Tbsp. vinegar
1 Tbsp. sugar
2 Tbsp. half and half
Pepper to taste

SERVES 4-6
Mix all ingredients together and let stand 20-30 minutes.

GLORIOUS CUCUMBER SALAD

2—3 oz. pkg. lime-flavored
  gelatin
1½ cups hot water
2 Tbsp. lemon juice
1½ medium cucumbers,
  unpeeled
1 large onion
1 pint creamed cottage
  cheese
1 cup pecans, chopped
2 cups mayonnaise

SERVES 10-12
Dissolve gelatin in hot water. Add lemon juice and cool. In a blender or food processor, grind cucumbers and onion. Strain off juice. Add cucumbers and onion to the gelatin mixture. Then stir in cottage cheese, pecans, and mayonnaise. Mix well. Pour into a 2 quart mold and chill until firm. Good served with chicken or seafood.

SALADS

CAULIFLOWER SALAD

1 head cauliflower, broken
  into buds
1 bunch green onions,
  sliced
1 bunch radishes, sliced
¾ lb. Monterey Jack or
  Longhorn cheese, grated
Pepperoni or ham, sliced
  or cubed into small
  pieces
¼-½ cup Italian dressing

SERVES 6
Layer ingredients in order given. Pour dressing over salad. Cover and let marinate 24 hours in refrigerator.

PEA-CAULIFLOWER SALAD

1—10 oz. pkg. frozen peas,
  cooked and drained
1 head cauliflower, broken
  into pieces
¼-½ cup celery, diced
¼-½ cup onion, diced
½-¾ cup mayonnaise (not
  salad dressing)

SERVES 4-6
Toss all ingredients together the day before serving. Refrigerate.

NEVA'S SALAD

1—8 oz. carton sour cream
¼ cup mayonnaise
3 tsp. vinegar
½ medium onion, minced
1 head cauliflower, broken
  into pieces
1 bunch fresh broccoli,
  broken into pieces
2 carrots, peeled and
  chopped
Salt and pepper to taste
Dash of Tabasco (about 3
  shakes)

SERVES 4-6
Mix all ingredients together the day before serving. Refrigerate.

MARINATED GREEN BEANS

2—20 oz. cans of green
   beans (Blue Lake),
   drained
1 thinly sliced onion
1 Tbsp. salad oil
1 Tbsp. vinegar
Salt and pepper to taste

SOUR CREAM SAUCE:
1 cup sour cream
1 tsp. lemon juice
½ to 1 Tbsp. horseradish
2 tsp. chopped chives
½ cup mayonnaise
¼ tsp. dry mustard
Grated onion to taste

SERVES 6
Combine beans, onion, oil, vinegar, salt and pepper. Let marinate several hours or overnight in the refrigerator. Stir occasionally. Drain. Add sour cream sauce.

To make sour cream sauce, combine all ingredients. Mix well and pour over green bean salad.

BEAN SALAD

1—1 lb. can green beans
1—1 lb. can yellow beans
1—1 lb. can red kidney
   beans
1—1 lb. can garbanzo
   beans (optional)
1—4 oz. can green lima
   beans (optional)
1 red onion, sliced or
   chopped
1 green pepper, sliced or
   chopped

DRESSING:
¾ cup sugar
¾ cup vinegar
¾ cup oil
1¼ Tbsp. dry mustard
1 tsp. salt
1 tsp. pepper

SERVES 8-10
Combine sugar, vinegar, oil and spices in a small saucepan. Bring to boil. Drain beans and combine in large bowl. Pour warm dressing over beans. Add onion and pepper. Stir well. Cover and refrigerate at least 3 hours, overnight is better. Stir occasionally.

SALADS

COPPER CARROT SALAD

2 lbs. carrots (canned),
  drained
1 green pepper, chopped
1 onion, chopped
1 cup tomato soup
½ cup salad oil
1 cup sugar
¾ cup vinegar
1 tsp. Worcestershire
Salt
Pepper
1 tsp. prepared mustard

SERVES 8
Alternate layers of carrots, pepper, and onion. Make a sauce with soup, oil, sugar, vinegar, Worcestershire, salt, pepper, and mustard. Heat until well blended. Pour hot mixture over vegetables and refrigerate several days before using. Will keep 3 weeks. You can also serve this salad as a vegetable by serving warm. It's good with chicken. Or try putting a few of the marinated carrots in a tossed green salad.

ZINGY V-8 ASPIC

1—3 oz. pkg. lemon gelatin
½ cup boiling water
1 cup V-8 juice
½ cup sliced pimento-
  stuffed olives
½ cup finely chopped
  celery
½ tsp. salt
1/8 tsp. Worcestershire
  sauce
Dash Tabasco sauce

SERVES 4-6
Dissolve gelatin in boiling water; cool. Mix in V-8, olives, and celery. Add salt, Worcestershire, and Tabasco to taste. Mix well. Pour into mold and refrigerate until set. This versatile salad complements any meal.

SARAH'S TOMATO ASPIC

1—1 lb. can stewed
   tomatoes
1—3 oz. pkg. lemon
   flavored gelatin
½ tsp. salt
1 Tbsp. vinegar

SERVES 5

Puree tomatoes in food processor or blender; pour into saucepan, saving the can. Bring tomatoes to a boil. Reduce heat; simmer for two minutes. Add gelatin, salt and vinegar; stir until gelatin dissolves. Pour into stewed tomato can. Chill until firm. Puncture bottom of can. Dip in warm water. Unmold on a bed of lettuce. This is a real hit at salad luncheons, and is also good with scrambled eggs at brunch, or with seafood.

MRS. WALKER'S COLE SLAW

Mix equal parts of vinegar, sour cream, and sugar (½ cup each for a big salad). Add shredded red and green cabbage.

CABBAGE PATCH COLE SLAW

5 cups shredded cabbage
1 cup sour cream
¼ cup white vinegar
½ cup vegetable oil
½ tsp. celery seed
½ tsp. salt
3 Tbsp. sugar

SERVES 6

Stir together dressing; pour over cabbage. Toss and chill.

SALADS

SAUERKRAUT SALAD

1 can sauerkraut (2½ cups)
⅓ cup sugar
½ cup green pepper, chopped
½ cup carrots, grated
½ cup onion, chopped
½ cup celery, chopped

SERVES 4-6
Drain juice from sauerkraut and add ⅓ cup sugar. Mix to dissolve sugar. Add other ingredients and stir well. Dill seed is also good to add. Let chill at least two hours before serving. Will keep for a couple of weeks in the refrigerator.

ZUCCHINI SALAD

1 medium zucchini, chopped
1 cup cheddar or Monterey Jack cheese, cubed or shredded
1 cup ham, salami or pepperoni, sliced or cubed
1 hard boiled egg, chopped
½ tomato, chopped

DRESSING:
½ cup oil
½ cup vinegar
¼ cup honey
¼ tsp. garlic, minced
¼ tsp. salt
Pepper
2 Tbsp. grated or minced onion
1½ Tbsp. fresh parsley

SERVES 4-6
Combine salad ingredients and toss well. Combine dressing ingredients in pint jar, shake well, and pour over salad. Toss before serving.

24-HOUR LAYERED VEGETABLE SALAD

6 cups lettuce, chopped
6 eggs, hard-boiled
1 lb. bacon, cooked and
   crumbled
Salt
Pepper
2 Tbsp. sugar
1—10 oz. pkg. frozen peas,
   thawed and uncooked
2 cups Swiss cheese,
   grated
¼ cup green onion,
   chopped
1 cup Miracle Whip salad
   dressing
Paprika

SERVES 12-15
Place 3 cups lettuce in bottom of large bowl; sprinkle with salt, pepper and sugar. Layer sliced eggs on top of lettuce and sprinkle with more salt. Layer in order: peas, remaining lettuce, bacon, and Swiss cheese. Spread salad dressing over top. Cover and chill 24 hours. Garnish with green onion and paprika. Toss before serving. This is especially pretty if served in a large crystal bowl. Makes a very large salad. You can also layer this salad in a 9 x 13 glass baking dish. Make sure to cover the entire top of the salad with the dressing as it seals the lettuce mixture and keeps it crisp. It will stay fresh for several days. Serve by cutting into squares.

WILTED LETTUCE SALAD

4 slices bacon, diced
¼ cup vinegar
2 tsp. sugar
¼ tsp. salt
1/8 tsp. pepper
1 large bunch leaf lettuce,
   torn into pieces
5 green onions with tops,
   chopped

SERVES 4
Fry bacon until crisp. Remove bacon from grease and set aside. Add vinegar, sugar, salt and pepper to bacon drippings. Tear lettuce into large mixing bowl, and add onion. Heat vinegar mixture to boiling. Pour over lettuce, tossing as you pour. Turn skillet upside down over bowl. Let set 5 minutes. Add bacon and serve immediately.

SALADS

SPINACH SALAD

1 pkg. fresh spinach
4 hard-boiled eggs, sliced
8 strips bacon
1 cup bean sprouts,
    drained
1 small can water
    chestnuts, diced

TANGY DRESSING:
1 cup salad oil
¼ cup wine vinegar
¾ cup sugar
½ tsp. salt
⅓ cup ketchup
2 tsp. Worcestershire sauce
½ onion, quartered

SERVES 6
Fry bacon until crisp. Drain thoroughly and crumble. Wash and drain spinach. Break into bite size pieces. Combine ingredients and toss carefully with Tangy Dressing.

Combine dressing ingredients in blender and puree.

RICH GREEN SALAD

1 head leaf lettuce, washed
    and dried
1—6 oz. jar marinated
    artichoke hearts, drained
    (save oil)
½ cup pitted ripe olives,
    sliced
Croutons
Parmesan cheese

DRESSING:
Juice of ½ lemon
1 tsp. dill weed
¼ cup olive oil
½ tsp. salt
Dash of pepper
Marinade from artichoke
    hearts

SERVES 6
Tear lettuce into small pieces. Cut olives and artichoke hearts into pieces and mix with lettuce. Toss with dressing just before serving; add croutons and Parmesan cheese to taste.

This salad is especially good with steak or prime rib but will complement any entree beautifully.

POTATO SALAD

6 potatoes (medium)
¼ cup red onion, finely
chopped
1 tsp. salt
1/8 tsp. pepper
¼ cup Italian salad
dressing
½ cup mayonnaise or salad
dressing
½ cup celery, chopped
4 eggs, hard-boiled,
chopped
1 tsp. celery seed

SERVES 6-8
Put unpared potatoes in boiling water, cover and cook until tender. Drain, cool and peel. Cut potatoes in cubes, combine with onion, salt and pepper. Add Italian dressing, cover and refrigerate 2-3 hours. Just before serving, add mayonnaise, celery, eggs, and celery seed. Toss well.

HOT GERMAN POTATO SALAD

2 lbs. potatoes (about 6)
6 slices bacon
1 medium onion, chopped
⅓ cup sugar
⅓ cup vinegar
⅓ cup water
1 tsp. celery seed
Salt
Pepper

SERVES 4
Boil potatoes in their skins. Cook bacon until crisp, then saute the onion in the bacon drippings. Peel cooked potatoes and cut into bite-sized pieces. (Also good with peelings left on.) Crumble bacon over potatoes. Heat bacon drippings, onion, vinegar, sugar, water and celery seed until boiling and pour over hot potatoes. Make sure liquid and potatoes are very hot when mixed together. Mix well. Add salt and pepper to taste, put into 2½ quart casserole and bake, uncovered, 30 minutes at 300°. You can prepare this ahead and refrigerate, as it does taste better the second day. Just be sure to serve it hot. Good with barbecued ribs or sausage.

Eggs that are several days old are best for boiling as they will peel easier.

SALADS

▼■▼■▼■▼■▼■▼■▼■▼■▼■▼■▼■▼■▼■▼■▼■▼■▼

ARTICHOKE RICE SALAD

1—6 oz. pkg. Chicken
   Rice-a-Roni
2—7 oz. jars marinated
   artichoke hearts
⅓ cup mayonnaise
¼ tsp. curry powder
12 pimento stuffed
   olives, sliced
½ green pepper, chopped
   fine
1 green onion, sliced
   (tops also)

SERVES 8-10

Cook Rice-a-Roni according to package directions. Cool. Drain artichoke hearts, reserving liquid. Combine reserved artichoke liquid and curry powder. Blend well. Add remaining ingredients and mix thoroughly. Chill. This is better if made a day in advance. For a variation, add chopped chicken or ham to make this salad a main course. Makes a large salad.

SOUTH OF THE BORDER SALAD

1 head lettuce, washed and
   drained
1 tomato, chopped
3-4 green onions, chopped
1 small can garbanzo beans
1 avocado, sliced
10 black olives, sliced
¾ cup hamburger, fried
¾ cup tortilla chips,
   slightly crushed
¼ cup cheddar cheese,
   grated
Thousand Island dressing

SERVES 4

Tear lettuce into small pieces. Add tomato, green onions, garbanzos, avocado, and olives. Fry hamburger and drain off grease. Just before serving, add hamburger, chips, and cheese. Add dressing and toss. Excellent with Beef Enchiladas.

 Place an avocado in cornmeal overnight to ripen.

ENSALADA MEXICANA

1 sweet red onion
2 tomatoes
2 small heads lettuce
   (Iceberg, Romaine, or
   leaf)
1 ripe avocado
8 black olives, sliced
1 lb. ground beef
1—1 lb. can Ranch style
   beans (you may
   substitute 1 cup of your
   own cooked pinto beans)
¼ tsp. salt
4 oz. cheddar cheese,
   grated
Tabasco sauce
10 oz. bag tortilla chips,
   slightly crushed
8 oz. bottle Western-style
   or red French dressing

SERVES 8-10
Chop onion, tomatoes, lettuce, avocado, and olives. Refrigerate. Brown ground beef and drain fat. Add beans, salt and a few shakes of Tabasco. Simmer about 15 minutes. When ready to serve, add beef and cheese to refrigerated items. Add crushed chips and toss with dressing. Serve immediately. You may want to add a few more shakes of Tabasco before serving. Makes a great main course meal, especially in the summer.

EASY GUACAMOLE

2 ripe avocados
½ tsp. lemon juice
3-4 Tbsp. Pace's Picante
   sauce
Garlic salt

SERVES 4
Mash 2 ripe avocados. Add lemon juice, Pace's Picante sauce, and some garlic salt to taste. Serve with tortilla chips or on top of burritos.

SALADS

CRAB LOUIS

3 cups canned crabmeat,
   drained, or frozen cooked
   crabmeat, thawed
3 tomatoes, quartered
4 hard-boiled eggs,
   quartered
5 cups lettuce, torn into
   bite-size pieces

DRESSING:
1½ cups mayonnaise or
   salad dressing
⅓ cup French dressing
⅓ cup chili sauce
2 Tbps. minced green
   onion or chives
2 Tbsp. chopped green
   olives
1 tsp. prepared horseradish
1 tsp. onion juice or
   grated onion
1 tsp. lemon juice
1 tsp. Worcestershire sauce
1/8 tsp. salt
1/8 tsp. pepper
Dash Tabasco

SERVES 4-5
Combine dressing ingredients. Mix thoroughly. On individual serving dishes, arrange crabmeat on lettuce with tomatoes and eggs. Pour dressing over salad. Crabmeat can be combined with the dressing, if you prefer.

TOMATOES AND CRABMEAT

2-3 large red tomatoes,
   sliced thick
1 can King Crabmeat,
   drained

RUSSIAN DRESSING:
½ cup oil
¼ cup wine vinegar
6 Tbsp. sugar
3 Tbsp. ketchup
1 tsp. salt

SERVES 4
Slice tomatoes. Mound King Crab on each slice, then dribble Russian dressing over each. Serve on a bed of lettuce. This is a good accompaniment to smoked ham or turkey.

MOLDED TUNA SALAD

3 hard-boiled eggs
1 pkg. unflavored gelatin,
   dissolved in ¼ cup cold
   water
1 family-size can tuna,
   drained
½ cup sliced green olives
¼ tsp. onion flakes
2-2½ cups mayonnaise

SERVES 6
Cook gelatin mixture in a double boiler until thin. Add mayonnaise and stir until creamy. Add tuna, eggs, olives, and onion flakes. Pour into mold or loaf pan, and chill. This makes a delicious luncheon dish. Serve with a fresh fruit salad.

CURRIED SHRIMP SALAD

1 lb. shrimp, cooked,
   shelled and chilled
1 cup celery, sliced
3 green onions, chopped
½ cup mayonnaise
½ cup sour cream
Juice of 1 lemon
1½ tsp. curry powder
1 tsp. salt
Pepper

SERVES 6
Cut shrimp in half, lengthwise; add celery and green onions. Mix remaining ingredients to make a sauce; add shrimp. Serve on bed of lettuce. For something different, serve this salad on avocado halves or with quartered tomatoes. Try substituting crabmeat for the shrimp. The curry sauce alone is a good dip for crudites

SALADS

TOSSED SHRIMP SALAD

1 bunch salad greens (bibb
   or leaf lettuce)
1½ cups frozen, fresh
   cocktail shrimp
2-3 hard-boiled eggs
1 avocado, sliced
12 cherry tomatoes, halved
1 cup broccoli flowerets
2 Tbsp. green onion,
   chopped
¼ cup celery, chopped
1 small can ripe olives,
   chopped
½ cup grated cheddar
   cheese
Russian or Western Style
   dressing

SERVES 4
Wash and drain lettuce. Tear into bite
sized pieces. Add other ingredients
and serve with Russian or Western
style dressing. This makes a delicious
summertime meal in itself.

ITALIAN SCROODLE SALAD

1—8 oz. pkg. scroodle
   macaroni, cooked and
   drained
1—3 oz. pkg. pepperoni,
   diced small (may
   substitute ham)
1½ cup Provolone cheese,
   shredded
3 green onions and tops,
   chopped
1 can garbanzo beans,
   (optional)
Italian dressing

SERVES 4-6
Cook scroodles as directed, rinse
with cold water and drain. Combine
with other ingredients. Pour dressing
over salad and mix well. Let chill 1-2
hours before serving.

SUMMERTIME MACARONI SALAD

3 cups cooked shell
  macaroni (1½ cups
  uncooked)
2 green onions, chopped
¼ cup pimento
1 small can black olives
  (may substitute ¼ cup
  sliced green olives for
  the pimento and black
  olives)
1 cup cheddar cheese,
  grated or cubed
¼ cup celery, chopped
¾ cup salad dressing or
  mayonnaise
½ tsp. salt
¼ tsp. pepper
Dash of garlic salt
2 tsp. celery seed

SERVES 6

Cook macaroni as directed. Drain and rinse with cold water. Combine macaroni with onion, pimento, olives, cheese, and celery. Mix mayonnaise with salt, pepper, garlic salt, and celery seed. Add to the macaroni mixture, blend well. Chill 3-4 hours.

Crack hard boiled eggs and let sit in cold water several minutes for easier peeling.

Meats

MEATS

BARBECUED BRISKET OR RIBS

1 ½ tsp. salt
1 ½ tsp. onion salt
3 tsp. celery salt
3 Tbsp. Worcestershire
  sauce
1 ½ tsp. pepper
4 Tbsp. liquid smoke
4-6 lbs. brisket or ribs
Hickory Barbecue Sauce
  (see recipe in sauce
  section)

SERVES 8-10
Combine all ingredients except barbecue sauce in a cup. Arrange brisket in foil. Pour salt mixture over brisket and marinate overnight. Bake wrapped in foil with marinade at 225° for 6-8 hours, depending on the size of brisket. Brisket is delicious with this juice or with barbecue sauce added during the last two hours of cooking. To cook ribs, marinate overnight as you would the brisket. Before baking, pour barbecue sauce generously over ribs and bake, covered tightly at 225° for 6 hours. Serve with Potato Salad, Cowboy Beans, and Texas Buttermilk Biscuits for a true western-style barbecue!

JOANIE'S MARINATED GRILLED STEAK

Juice of one lemon
½ cup soy sauce
3 Tbsp. vegetable oil
2 Tbsp. Worcestershire
  sauce
1 clove garlic, minced
Pepper
Chopped green onion
2 lb. flank steak

SERVES 4
Mix all ingredients in the pan in which meat is to be marinated. Marinate steak, turning occasionally, for 4-12 hours in refrigerator. Broil meat over hot coals to desired doneness.

 Low cooking temperature keeps the juice and flavor in the meat, cuts down on shrinkage, and keeps the meat more tender.

STEAK DIANA

¼ cup butter
1 cup fresh mushrooms,
   sliced
2 Tbsp. minced green
   onion
1/8 tsp. garlic powder
1/8 tsp. salt
1 tsp. lemon juice
1 tsp. Worcestershire sauce
1½ Tbsp. parlsey, chopped
2 Tbsp. butter
1¼ lb. beef tenderloin, cut
   in 2 inch slices

SERVES 4
Melt butter in skillet, add mushrooms, onion, garlic, salt, lemon juice, and Worcestershire sauce. Cook until mushrooms are tender. Add parsley. Pour in small bowl. In skillet melt another 2 tablespoons butter. Cook tenderloin over medium-high heat, 3-4 minutes on each side. Pour mushroom-butter mixture over meat in skillet. Heat thoroughly. Remove from heat, cover and let sit 10-15 minutes, to allow flavors to blend. Heat again to serve. Delicious with Cattlemen's Club Twice Baked Potatoes, green salad and Mud Pie for dessert.

UNATTENDED RIB ROAST

1 standing rib roast,
   any size
Salt and pepper

Preheat oven to 375° 6-7 hours before mealtime. Season roast with salt and pepper and place in roasting pan. Cook, uncovered for 1 hour, then turn off oven. DO NOT OPEN OVEN DOOR. Turn heat on again to 375° 40 minutes before serving. The roast will be medium rare in the center and well done around the edges.

MEATS

BEST EVER POT ROAST

3-4 lb. arm roast
2 cups water
Lawry's seasoned salt
Pepper
1 bay leaf (optional)
6 potatoes, pared and cut
in pieces
6-8 carrots, peeled and cut
in pieces
2 onions, quartered

GRAVY:
3-4 Tbsp. cornstarch
½ cup water
½ tsp. salt
¼ tsp. pepper
1 tsp. Kitchen Bouquet

SERVES 6
Set pot roast in roasting pan, sprinkle liberally with salt and pepper. Add 2 cups water and bay leaf; cover and cook in 250° oven 5-6 hours. About an hour before supper, add vegetables and turn up oven to 325°. In an hour's time you will have a tender, moist pot roast and vegetables with a minimum of fuss. (You can even put the roast in frozen, only do it an hour or so earlier.) Remove meat and vegetables from roaster and set pan on stove top to make gravy. While stirring constantly over medium high heat, add enough cornstarch, dissolved in cold water, to drippings to make desired consistency. Season with salt, pepper and Kitchen Bouquet.

SWISS STEAK

1 arm roast (4 lbs.)
¼ cup flour
½ tsp. salt
¼ tsp. garlic powder
Pepper
2-3 Tbsp. oil
1—16 oz. can tomatoes,
cut up
1 onion, sliced
1 small green pepper,
sliced

SERVES 6
Heat oil in large skillet. Season roast with salt, pepper, and garlic powder. Dredge in flour, then brown on both sides in hot oil. Place in roasting pan. Arrange onion and pepper slices on top of roast, then pour tomatoes over top. Cover and bake at 250° for at least 4 hours, more if you have time. Check occasionally to see if it needs water. Makes its own gravy when cooked like this and is so tender it cuts like butter!

SHISH-KA-BOB

1 sirloin steak (about
  2 lbs.), cut into cubes
Italian dressing

Vegetable/Fruit Ideas:
  (Use at least three
  different ones)
Cherry tomatoes (about 10)
Green pepper, quartered (3)
Onion, quartered (3)
Pineapple chunks
Whole mushrooms
Corn on the cob, 2 inch
  pieces

SERVES 4-6
Marinate steak cubes in Italian dressing 4-6 hours in refrigerator. On skewer put pieces of steak alternating with the other selections. Ex: steak, mushroom, tomato, pineapple, steak, etc. This will fill about 4 skewers. Grill outside on charcoal cooker until meat is desired doneness. Serve with Easy Rice, Spinach Salad, and Braided Potato Bread.

EASY BEEF STROGANOFF

1 lb. sirloin steak, cut into
  small cubes or ½ inch
  strips
½ cup flour
3 Tbsp. oil
1/8 tsp. garlic powder
1 pint beef bouillon
1 can cream of mushroom
  soup
1 cup sliced mushrooms
¾ cup sour cream
3-4 cups noodles, cooked
  and drained
Parsley

SERVES 4
Cut steak into cubes or strips. Put ½ cup flour and garlic powder in plastic bag, add meat, and shake to coat meat well. Heat oil in large skillet. Saute meat and mushrooms over medium heat, stirring occasionally. When meat coating is crispy, pour in bouillon and mushroom soup. Mix well. Simmer 20-30 minutes, stirring occasionally. Before serving, stir in sour cream and heat through. Serve over hot noodles. Garnish with parsley.

Pierce an onion with a fork before cooking. It will retain its shape without falling apart.

MEATS

CHICKEN FRIED STEAK & CREAM GRAVY

4 cubed steaks or round steak (pound round steak well with mallet or sharp knife)
2 eggs
½-¾ cup flour
Oil
Salt and pepper
6 Tbsp. flour
3 cups milk

SERVES 4
Pound steak well. Divide steak into portion size pieces. Dip into beaten egg, then coat with flour. Pour 1/8 inch oil in bottom of skillet. Have grease fairly hot before putting in steaks. Let fry on one side until well browned, about 4 minutes. Season with salt and pepper. Keeping heat fairly hot, turn steak to brown other side. Place steak on dish and set in 250° oven while making gravy.

To make gravy, drain or add enough oil to have 2-3 tablespoons of grease in pan. Add 6 tablespoons flour and stir well to loosen crumbs on bottom and blend in flour. Add milk slowly, stirring constantly until gravy is desired consistency. Serve with fried or mashed potatoes, Okra and Tomatoes, and Fresh Strawberry Pie for dessert. Wow!

STEAK AND POTATOES

Round steak (1½-2 lbs.)
Meat tenderizer
½-¾ cup flour
3 Tbsp. oil
Lawry's seasoned salt
Pepper
1 can cream of onion soup
1 can cream of mushroom soup
Potatoes, peeled and sliced (as many as your family eats)

SERVES 4-5
Sprinkle steak with meat tenderizer and let sit ½-1 hour. Cut steak into single portion pieces and dredge each in flour. Brown on both sides in oil. Season meat with seasoned salt and pepper as it cooks. Remove browned meat and drain on paper towel. Put soups and 1 soup can of milk into frying pan and mix with crusties from meat. Stir well. Grease a 3 quart casserole and layer meat, potatoes, and gravy, ending with gravy. Bake, covered, at 300° for 3-4 hours. This makes a delicious one-pot meal, made early in the day and ready to eat at suppertime. Good with hot biscuits.

CORNED BEEF & CABBAGE

4 lbs. corned beef
1 onion
3-4 potatoes, chunked
3 carrots
3-4 rutabagas (optional)
½-¾ head cabbage, cut in thin wedges

SERVES 8
Place corned beef in large kettle or crockpot. Cover with water. Slice onion and place around beef. Cook all day in crockpot or simmer at least 5-6 hours in kettle. An hour before serving, add carrots, potatoes and rutabagas. Cook 45 minutes; then add cabbage. Simmer until cabbage is tender, about 15-20 minutes. Serve with Irish Soda Bread and Blarney Stones for dessert, and you've got a real St. Patrick's Day feast!

BEEF JERKY

1 lb. flank steak
1 tsp. seasoned salt
½ tsp. garlic powder
½ tsp. onion powder
¼ tsp. pepper
⅓ cup soy sauce
⅓ cup Worcestershire sauce
2 Tbsp. liquid smoke

Pat flank steak dry and slice thinly across grain of meat. In a plastic bag, combine rest of ingredients. Place meat in bag, making sure each slice is coated with marinade. Place in refrigerator overnight. Drain meat on paper towels, blotting well. Place meat on oven rack and cook at 140° for 3 hours. It helps to open the oven door a crack to let moisture escape. Put a piece of foil on oven floor to catch any drippings. Keep in a jar in the refrigerator and watch them disappear!

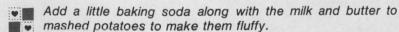 *Add a little baking soda along with the milk and butter to mashed potatoes to make them fluffy.*

MEATS

LAZY LADY STEW

2 lbs. cubed stew meat
1—1 lb. can tiny peas (may
   substitute 1—10 oz. pkg.
   frozen peas)
1 cup sliced carrots
2 onions, chopped
2 potatoes, pared and
   sliced
1 tsp. salt
Dash of pepper
1 can cream of tomato soup
½ soup can water
1 bay leaf

SERVES 4

Mix all ingredients in a large casserole. Cook, covered, in a 275°
oven for 6 hours. The stew meat can
be put in frozen, but increase the
cooking time by 1 hour. Not only is
this stew delicious, but it is un-
believably easy. Serve with Homestyle Cornbread and a green salad.
(You can easily double or triple these
proportions and feed a crowd.)

HEARTY HODGEPODGE

6 slices bacon
1 medium onion, thinly
   sliced
1 lb. beef shank
¾ lb. ham hock
6 cups water
2 tsp. salt
2—15 oz. cans garbanzo
   beans
3 cups potatoes, diced
1/8 tsp. garlic powder
6 oz. polish sausage,
   thinly sliced

SERVES 4-6

In large heavy kettle, cook bacon until
crisp. Reserve 2 tablespoons drippings. Crumble bacon and set aside.
Saute onion in bacon drippings until
tender. Add beef shank, ham hock,
water, and salt. Cover and simmer 1½
hours. Remove meat from shank and
ham hock; dice. Skim fat from broth.
Return diced meat to soup; add undrained beans, potatoes and garlic.
Simmer, covered for 30 minutes. Add
sausage and bacon. Simmer covered,
15 minutes longer. This is a delicious
stew type meal. Serve with Sourdough Bread.

ZELDA'S CABBAGE ROLLS

1½ lbs. ground beef
½ cup rice
½ tsp. salt
½ tsp. pepper
¾-1 tsp. garlic powder
1 onion, diced
1 egg
1 head cabbage

SAUCE:
2—6 oz. cans tomato sauce
Juice of two lemons
3 Tbsp. flour (rounded)
½ cup sugar

SERVES 4-6
Mix ground beef with rice, salt, pepper, garlic powder, onion, and egg. Dunk cabbage leaves in boiling water to make pliable. Place ¼ cup hamburger mixture on each leaf and wrap. Makes about 12 rolls. Combine ingredients to make sauce. There are several ways to cook these, the best being in a pressure cooker.

Pressure Cooker Method: Heat sauce in the pressure pan. Place cabbage rolls in sauce. Cover and seal. Heat slowly until pressure is on 10 lbs. Cook 10 minutes.

Crockpot Method: Pour half the sauce in the bottom of the crock pot, then add cabbage rolls. Pour remaining sauce over rolls. Cover and cook on high 5-6 hours.

Oven Method: Place rolls in a large greased baking dish. Spoon sauce over rolls and cover dish tightly. Bake at 325° for 1-1½ hours. Check every 20-30 minutes to see if extra liquid is needed. Add water accordingly.

MEATS

CORNY SANDWICH SQUARES

CORNBREAD:
1 cup yellow cornmeal
1 cup white flour
¼ cup sugar
½ tsp. salt
4 tsp. baking powder
1 egg
1 cup milk
¼ cup vegetable oil
1—4 oz. can cream-style
   corn
¾ cup Velveeta, grated

FILLING:
1 lb. ground beef, browned
¼-½ cup ketchup
2 Tbsp. sweet pickle relish
½ cup Velveeta, grated
¼ cup Parmesan cheese

SAUCE:
¼ cup cold water
1 Tbsp. cornstarch
1—16 oz. can stewed
   tomatoes, cut up
1 tsp. Worcestershire sauce

SERVES 6

Mix cornbread ingredients, adding cream-style corn and ¾ cup cheese. Spread half the batter in a greased 8x8x2 baking pan. In a skillet, brown ground beef, drain off fat. Add ketchup and relish to meat and spread on batter. Sprinkle with ½ cup Velveeta, and the Parmesan. Top with remaining batter. Bake at 350° for 45-55 minutes. Let stand 5 minutes before cutting.

Prepare the sauce by combining water and cornstarch in small saucepan. Stir in tomatoes and Worcestershire. Cook and stir until mixture thickens and bubbles. Serve over cornbread squares. This is an unusual and really delicious meal.

 When freezing a casserole dish, line your casserole with foil before filling it, then freeze. When it's frozen solid, slip food and foil from the casserole dish, seal tightly and replace in freezer. The dish can be used while the casserole waits. When ready to bake, slip food from foil, place casserole in the same dish and bake.

MEATS

HAMBURGER-SOUR CREAM CASSEROLE

1½ lbs. hamburger
1 onion, chopped
¼ green pepper, chopped
1 can cream of chicken
  soup
1 can cream of mushroom
  soup
1—12 oz. can corn niblets,
  drained
3 cups cooked noodles
  (5 oz.)
1 cup sour cream
½ tsp. salt
¼ tsp. pepper
1—3 oz. can chow mein
  noodles

SERVES 6
In a skillet combine meat, onions, and pepper and brown slowly; drain fat. Add all ingredients except chow mein noodles. Place in a 9 x 13 inch baking dish and top with chow mein noodles. Bake, uncovered, for 25-30 minutes at 350°. Freezes well, but do not put chow mein noodles on top until ready to bake.

GOLDEN BEEF CASSEROLE

2 lbs. lean ground beef
1 medium onion, chopped
½ green pepper, chopped
1—1 lb. can tomatoes
3 Tbsp. ketchup
1 Tbsp. chili powder
1 Tbsp. Heinz 57 steak
  sauce
5 oz. macaroni, cooked and
  drained
½ cup sharp cheddar
  cheese, grated
1 can Golden Mushroom
  soup
Salt and pepper to taste

SERVES 6-8
Brown meat, onions, and green pepper. Drain fat. Add tomatoes, ketchup, steak sauce, chili powder, salt and pepper. Cook, covered, about 30 minutes. Pour mixture into casserole. Add cooked macaroni, stir in mushroom soup and top with grated cheese. Bake, uncovered, at 350° about 30 minutes.

MEATS

TEXAS HASH

1 lb. ground beef
1 large onion, chopped
1 large green pepper,
    chopped
1—1 lb. can tomatoes,
    cut up
½ cup uncooked regular
    rice
2 tsp. chili powder
2 tsp. salt
1/8 tsp. pepper

SERVES 4-6

In large skillet, brown beef, onion, and green pepper. Drain fat. Add tomatoes, rice, chili powder, salt and pepper. Heat through. Pour into 2 quart casserole, cover and bake 1 hour at 350°. You can put this in the microwave if in a hurry and cook on high, turning every 10 minutes for 25 minutes. This is easy, fast, and a hit with the whole family.

MEAT LOAF

2 lbs. ground beef
¼ lb. salt pork, chopped
    fine (leave this out if
    you don't happen to
    have it)
2 eggs, slightly beaten
1 cup milk
3 Tbsp. melted butter
1 Tbsp. horseradish
2 Tbsp. onion, minced
¼ tsp. pepper
¾ Tbsp. salt
1 cup soft bread crumbs
2 strips bacon

SERVES 8

Mix all ingredients, except the bacon and pack into greased loaf pan. Cover with strips of bacon and bake at 350° for 1 hour. Drain fat from meat loaf as soon as you remove from oven.

 Meatloaf will not stick to its pan if you place a strip of bacon at the bottom of the pan before placing your meatloaf in it.

HOMEMADE PIZZA

DOUGH:
1 pkg. dry yeast
1 cup lukewarm water
1 Tbsp. sugar
1 tsp. salt
2 Tbsp. oil
2½-3 cups flour

TOPPINGS:
1 jar Ragu Pizza Quick
  sauce
¾ lb. mozzarella cheese,
  grated
Pepperoni, sliced
Italian sausage, crumbled
  and browned
Sliced mushrooms, sauteed
Green pepper, diced
Sliced onions

MAKES 2 MEDIUM PIZZAS
In bowl dissolve yeast in warm water. Add sugar, salt and oil. Mix well. Gradually add flour to form a stiff dough. Knead on floured surface until smooth. Place in bowl, cover with a damp towel and let rise until doubled.

Divide dough in half and roll to ¼ inch thickness. Put each round in a medium size cast-iron skillet or pizza pan. Cover with Ragu sauce, grated cheese, then the toppings of your choice. Bake at 400° about 15 minutes or until golden.

PORCUPINE MEATBALLS

1 cup minute rice
1 egg, beaten
1 lb. ground beef
2 tsp. salt
2 tsp. grated onion
Pepper to taste
2½ cups tomato juice
½ tsp. sugar

SERVES 4
Mix ingredients except 2 cups tomato juice and sugar. Shape into meatballs and brown in skillet. Blend remaining juice and sugar. Pour in skillet with meatballs and bring to a boil. Cover and simmer slowly 15-20 minutes. Sprinkle with parsley if desired. Kids love these.

MEATS

SALISBURY STEAK

1½ lbs. ground beef
2 Tbsp. grated onion
1 tsp. salt
¼ tsp. dried marjoram
  leaves, crushed
1/8 tsp. pepper
1 envelope brown gravy mix
1—3 oz. can sliced
  mushrooms, drained
3 Tbsp. red wine (optional)

SERVES 4-6
Combine ground beef, grated onion, salt, marjoram, and pepper; mix well. Divide meat into six portions and shape into patties ¾ inch thick. Broil for 4-5 minutes on each side or until done. Prepare gravy mix according to package directions. Stir in mushrooms. Add wine if desired. Set patties in gravy. Remove from heat and let sit 20-30 minutes to allow flavors to blend. Simmer 5-10 minutes before serving. This is delicious with Italian Green Beans, baked potato and Peach Cobbler for dessert.

SHEPHERD'S PIE

1 lb. ground beef
1 onion, chopped
1—10 oz. can Rotel
  tomatoes
Salt and pepper
1—16 oz. can mixed
  vegetables, drained
4 medium potatoes, cooked
  and mashed
¾ cup cheddar cheese,
  grated

SERVES 4-6
Brown ground beef and onion. Drain grease. In casserole, combine Rotel tomatoes, salt, pepper, mixed vegetables and beef mixture. Top with mashed potatoes and grated cheese. Cook, uncovered at 350° until cheese melts, about 15-20 minutes. Freezes well.

 Try boiling potatoes (unpeeled) for about five minutes, then baking them in a hot oven. They will be thoroughly done in about one-half the usual time.

TEXAS RED CHILI

1 lb. ground beef
1 medium onion, chopped
1½ Tbsp. chili powder
1¼ tsp. salt
¼ tsp. garlic powder
¼ tsp. black pepper
1/8 tsp. ground cumin
1 Tbsp. vinegar
1—1 lb. can tomato sauce
2 cups water
2 cups pinto beans, cooked
(or 1 can Ranch Style
beans if you don't have
any pinto beans cooked
up)

SERVES 4

In a Dutch oven, brown ground beef and onion. Drain off fat. Add vinegar and seasonings. Stir well. Add tomato sauce, beans and water. Simmer over low heat 30 minutes. If you prefer thick chili, put 2 tablespoons flour in a jar, add ½ cup water, cover, and shake until mixed. Pour into chili and stir well. Serve with slices of Longhorn cheese, cold crisp apple, and Mexican Cornbread. The next day put it on hot dogs for a real Coney Island dog!

WEST OF THE PECOS

2 lbs. ground meat
1 large onion, chopped
1 green pepper, chopped
1—4 oz. can sliced
mushrooms
2 tsp. chili powder
¼ cup Worcestershire
sauce
1 tsp. salt
¼ tsp. pepper
1 can tomato soup
1—10 oz. can Rotel
tomatoes
1—16 oz. can cream-style
corn
1—12 oz. pkg. noodles,
cooked and drained
½ cup Longhorn cheese,
grated

SERVES 8-10

In large Dutch oven, brown ground beef, onion, and green pepper. Drain fat. Add mushrooms, chili powder, Worcestershire sauce, salt and pepper. Mix thoroughly. Add can of soup, tomatoes, and corn. Simmer ½ hour. Add cooked noodles, stir well. Top with grated cheese and bake, covered, 1 hour at 325°. This is an extra good goulash. Freezes well.

GREEN CHILI BURRITOS

SAUCE:
1½ lbs. cooked pork roast, cubed
1—10½ oz. can chicken broth
1—16 oz. can tomatoes, cut up
1—8 oz. can tomato sauce
¼-½ tsp. garlic powder
2—7 oz. cans diced green chilies
¼ oz. diced hot peppers
1 tsp. sugar
1 tsp. salt
2 Tbsp. flour, dissolved in ¼ cup water

FILLING:
1 lb. ground beef
¼-½ onion, diced
1 or 2—16 oz. cans refried beans

TOPPING:
Grated cheddar cheese
Shredded lettuce
Tomato, chopped
Sour cream

White flour tortillas

SERVES 4-6

Simmer pork in broth 5-10 minutes. Add canned tomatoes, tomato sauce, garlic, green chilies, hot peppers, sugar and salt. Let simmer 45 minutes. Thicken slightly with flour.

Brown hamburger and onion; drain grease. Add refried beans and blend together over low heat. Wrap flour tortillas in foil and warm in oven.

To serve: spoon bean and hamburger mixture on warm tortilla. Roll up tortilla and top with chili sauce. Sprinkle with cheese, lettuce and tomato. Top with spoonful of sour cream. The chili sauce freezes well.

BEEF ENCHILADAS

SAUCE:
1 medium onion, minced
2 Tbsp. vegetable oil
2 Tbsp. flour
2 cups chicken broth
¼ tsp. garlic powder
1—4 oz. can chopped, mild green chilies
2 cups canned tomatoes, drained and chopped

FILLING:
1 lb. ground beef
½ onion, chopped
1 tsp. chili powder
1 tsp. vinegar
½ tsp. salt
12 corn tortillas
2 cups grated Longhorn cheese

SERVES 6

Saute onion in oil until soft. Stir in flour and cook for 1 minute. Add broth and garlic powder, cook until thickened. Add chilies and tomatoes and simmer for 10 minutes. Puree sauce in blender or food processor.

Brown meat in large skillet with onion. Drain fat. Add vinegar, chili powder, and salt.

Dip each tortilla in sauce to soften it. Place a large spoonful of meat, a little grated cheese, and a spoonful of sauce in each. Roll up. Place in baking dish (seam side down) and repeat with remaining tortillas. Pour remaining sauce over all, top with cup of grated cheese and bake uncovered at 350° for 15-20 minutes. Serve with Easy Guacamole Salad, tortilla chips, Cowboy Beans, and a mug of frosty beer! This sauce freezes nicely, as do the enchiladas.

MEATS

TAMALE PIE

1 cup onion, chopped
1 lb. ground beef
2—8 oz. cans tomato sauce
1—12 oz. can whole kernel
    corn, drained
1 cup ripe olives, chopped
1/8 tsp. garlic powder
1 Tbsp. sugar
1 tsp. salt
2-3 tsp. chili powder
Dash of pepper
1½ cups Longhorn cheese,
    grated

TOPPING:
¾ cup yellow cornmeal
½ tsp. salt
2 cups cold water
1 Tbsp. butter

SERVES 6

In large skillet, brown beef and onion. Drain grease. Add tomato sauce, corn, olives, garlic, sugar, salt, chili powder, and pepper. Simmer about 20 minutes or until thick. Add cheese. Stir until cheese is melted. Pour into a greased 6 x 10 inch baking dish.

To make topping, stir cornmeal and salt into cold water. Stir over medium-low heat until thickened, about 3-4 minutes. Add butter and mix well. Spoon over meat mixture. Bake 40 minutes in 375° oven or until topping is browned.

FANCY TOSTADAS

1—16 oz. can refried beans
Dash Tabasco
¼ cup sliced green onion
4 oz. Monterey Jack
    cheese, grated
1 tomato, chopped
3 cups shredded lettuce
3 green onions, chopped
1 avocado, chopped
3 Tbsp. Italian salad
    dressing (Thousand
    Island is good also)
1 lb. ground beef
1 small onion, chopped
1/8 tsp. garlic powder
1—4 oz. can green chilies
1 can mild enchilada sauce
½ cup tomato juice
7-8 fried tortillas

SERVES 4

Combine refried beans, Tabasco, green onion and Monterey Jack cheese in small bowl. Cover and bake for 25 minutes at 325°. In salad bowl, combine tomato, lettuce, onion, and salad dressing. Brown ground beef, onion and garlic in skillet. Drain grease. Add green chilies, enchilada sauce and tomato juice. Mix well and let simmer 20 minutes. To serve: fry tortillas in ½ inch of oil in small skillet. Turn once. Top with hot refried bean mixture, meat sauce, then salad. Can top with cheese or taco sauce.

EGGPLANT PARMESAN

1 lb. ground beef
½ cup onion, chopped
1/8 tsp. garlic powder
1—16 oz. can tomatoes,
   cut up
1—6 oz. can tomato paste
½ tsp. salt
Pepper
¾ Tbsp. Italian seasoning
½ tsp. crushed cayenne
   red pepper
1½ Tbsp. brown sugar
2 small eggplants
¾ cup cracker crumbs
1 egg
8 oz. mozzarella cheese
¾ cup Parmesan cheese

SERVES 6

Brown hamburger, onion and garlic in saucepan. Drain grease. Add cut up tomatoes, tomato paste, salt, pepper, seasoning, red pepper, and sugar to meat. Let simmer ½-1 hour. Peel and slice eggplant. Beat egg. Dip eggplant slices in egg and then cracker crumbs. Melt butter in skillet and brown both sides of eggplant slices. Grease 9 x 13 inch casserole. Arrange eggplant slices in the bottom. Top with tomato mixture. Sprinkle mozzarella and Parmesan cheese over top. Bake uncovered 25 minutes at 350°. Serve with tossed green salad and French bread.

BOB AND GAYLE'S SPAGHETTI SAUCE

1 onion, chopped
1½ lbs. Italian sausage
2—1 lb. cans stewed
   tomatoes
1—8 oz. can tomato sauce
1—6 oz. can tomato paste
¼ cup cooking burgundy
Garlic powder to taste
1 tsp. leaf basil
1 tsp. leaf marjoram
1 tsp. leaf oregano

SERVES 4

Crumble sausage in large skillet and brown along with onion. Drain fat. Add other ingredients and simmer for 45 minutes to 1 hour. Serve over cooked and drained spaghetti with tossed green salad and garlic bread.

 Add a little cooking oil to boiling water when making spaghetti to keep it from sticking together. It should also keep the pot from boiling over.

MEATS

LASAGNA

2 lbs. ground beef
½ cup onion, chopped
Garlic salt
1—8 oz. can tomato sauce
1—6 oz. can tomato paste
1—20 oz. can tomatoes,
  cut up
1 tsp. oregano
2 tsp. salt
½ tsp. pepper
1 tsp. sweet basil
1 bay leaf

CHEESE FILLING:
3 cups cottage cheese
½ cup Parmesan cheese
2 Tbsp. parsley flakes
2 beaten eggs
½ tsp. pepper

1 lb. mozzarella cheese,
  grated
1—8 oz. pkg. lasagna
  noodles, cooked and
  drained

SERVES 9-12
Brown ground beef, onion, and garlic salt in large heavy skillet. Drain fat. Add tomato sauce, tomato paste, tomatoes, oregano, salt, pepper, sweet basil, and bay leaf and simmer 20 minutes.

Combine cheese filling ingredients and mix well. In a 9 x 13 inch pan, layer the noodles, meat sauce, cheese filling and mozzarella cheese; then repeat. Bake uncovered at 375° for 30 minutes. Let stand 10 minutes before serving. This is better if made the day before, refrigerated, and then baked. Allow some extra baking time if it has been refrigerated. If you are making this for your family, make two small pans and freeze one.

HAM AND POTATO BAKE

2 Tbsp. onion, chopped
½ cup margarine
½ cup flour
1 tsp. salt
½ tsp. dry mustard
Pepper
1½ cups milk
2 cups cheddar cheese
  grated
½ lb. ham, cut into cubes
  or 1/8 inch slices
6 cups cooked potato,
  sliced

SERVES 6
Saute onion in margarine. Blend in flour and seasonings. Gradually add milk, stirring constantly until thickened. Add 1½ cups cheese, stir until melted. Toss potatoes in cheese sauce. Layer the potato mixture and ham in a buttered casserole. Bake, uncovered, at 350° for 30 minutes. Top with remaining ½ cup cheese. Return to oven until melted.

■♥■♥■♥■♥■♥■♥■♥■♥■♥■♥■♥■♥■♥■♥■♥■♥■♥■

COMPANY CASSEROLE

24 oz. Jimmy Dean sausage
1 medium onion, chopped
1 cup green pepper,
   chopped
1 cup celery, chopped
1 cup uncooked rice
1 can chicken gumbo soup
2 cans cream of mushroom
   soup
1 cup mushrooms, sliced
2 cups water (including
   liquid from mushrooms)
1½ cups sharp cheddar
   cheese, grated
½ cup slivered almonds

SERVES 6-8
Brown sausage, onion, celery, and pepper in a large skillet. Drain grease. Add remaining ingredients. Spoon into large casserole. Bake, covered, at 350° for 1½ hours.

PORK CHOP POTATO SUPPER

4-5 pork chops
1—16 oz. can green beans,
   partially drained
2 cans cream of mushroom
   soup
3 potatoes, peeled, cut into
   fourths
Salt and pepper

SERVES 4-5
Mix green beans, soup, salt, pepper, and potatoes in small roasting pan. Nestle pork chops into mixture. Bake covered at 350° for 1½ hours.

HAM N' BEANS

2 cups dried lima beans
   or Great Northern beans,
   washed well
1 tsp. salt
1/8 tsp. pepper
2 cups ham, cut in pieces

SERVES 4-6
Soak beans overnight in 6 cups of water. Drain and put in pot with 6 cups of water. Season with salt and pepper. Add ham, and simmer over low heat for 2-3 hours, or until beans are tender. Serve with cornbread and a relish tray of green onions and Deviled Eggs.

MEATS

MILE HIGH PORK CHOP CASSEROLE

4 pork chops
2 Tbsp. oil
1 cup whole grain rice
1 tomato, sliced
1 green pepper, sliced
1 onion, sliced
1 can consomme
Salt and pepper, to taste

SERVES 4

Season pork chops with salt and pepper. In 2 tablespoons oil, brown pork chops on both sides in a skillet. Sprinkle rice in the bottom of a casserole. Lay pork chops on top of rice. Place a slice of onion, green pepper, and tomato on each pork chop. Pour consomme over all. Bake at 350°, covered, for 1½ hours, or until pork chops are tender and rice has absorbed all the moisture.

DARN GOOD BEANS

2 lbs. pinto beans
6 bouillon cubes (beef or chicken)
2-3 lbs. German sausage, cut up (you can substitute Polish or country-style)
3 Tbsp. Worcestershire sauce
1 jalapeno pepper, fresh (you may substitute sliced canned jalapenos)
2 onions, chopped
1 green pepper, chopped
1/8 tsp. garlic powder
1—1 lb. can tomato sauce
Salt to taste

SERVES AN ARMY (really 12-15)

Soak beans overnight. First thing in the morning, drain water from beans, put in a large Dutch oven, cover with fresh water and begin cooking over low heat. Slice sausage very thin, dice all vegetables and spices. Add everything to beans and cook over low heat all day, stirring frequently and adding water as necessary to prevent burning. (You can cook these in a crockpot on high.) Add salt to taste. For thicker bean soup, add 3 tablespoons flour mixed with ½ cup water at least 1 hour before beans are done. These are excellent as is, or spooned over cooked rice and served with hot buttered cornbread.

SWEET AND SOUR PORK

2 lbs. pork loins or shoulder, cut into 1 inch cubes
¾ cup flour
1 Tbsp. ginger
½ cup oil
1—13½ oz. can pineapple chunks, drained, reserve juice
½ cup vinegar
½ cup soy sauce
1 Tbsp. Worcestershire sauce
¾ cup sugar
2 tsp. salt
½ tsp. pepper
1 green pepper, cut into strips
1 can bean sprouts, drained
1 or 2 cans water chestnuts, sliced and drained
1 Tbsp. chili sauce
5 cups cooked rice

SERVES 6

Mix flour and ginger in plastic bag. Add pork cubes and shake well to coat. Heat oil in skillet. Add pork and brown on all sides. Remove meat from pan. Add enough water to the pineapple syrup to measure 1¾ cup. Add remaining flour from bag to skillet and stir. Add water/syrup mixture. Mix until smooth. Add vinegar, soy sauce and Worcestershire sauce. Heat to boiling, stirring constantly. Stir in sugar, salt, pepper and meat. Simmer 1 hour, covered. Add pineapple and green pepper. Cook, uncovered, 10 minutes. Stir in bean sprouts, water chestnuts and chili sauce. Cook 5 more minutes. Serve over hot rice.

 Rice grains stay white and separated if you add a teaspoon of lemon juice to each quart of cooking water.

MEATS

SUKIYAKI

2 Tbsp. cooking oil
1 lb. beef tenderloin,
   sliced thinly across the
   grain
2 Tbsp. sugar
½ cup beef broth
⅓ cup soy sauce
2 cups green onions,
   bias-sliced
1 cup celery, bias-sliced
1—16 oz. can bean sprouts,
   drained
1 cup mushrooms, thinly
   sliced
1—5 oz. can water
   chestnuts, drained and
   thinly sliced
1—5 oz. can bamboo
   shoots, drained
Hot cooked rice

SERVES 4

Heat oil in large skillet or wok. Add beef and cook quickly, turning meat over and over just until browned. Sprinkle with sugar. Combine broth and soy sauce and pour over meat. Push meat to one side. Let soy mixture bubble. In the Japanese style, keep the vegetables in separate groups as you cook them. Add onions, then celery, stir-frying each group over high heat about 1 minute, then pushing aside. Add the other vegetables in separate groups, stir-frying each just until heated through. You don't have to use each of these vegetables to make sukiyaki. You may substitute spinach, snow peas or zucchini, for any of the vegetables mentioned. Serve with hot cooked rice and extra soy sauce. If you are daring and want to try sukiyaki the Japanese way, dip each biteful in beaten raw egg before you eat it. It is really a taste treat!

Chicken
&
Fish

FRIED CHICKEN AND GRAVY

1 large fryer, cut up
3 eggs, beaten
1 cup flour
1-1½ tsp. salt
¼ tsp. pepper
½ tsp. paprika
½ tsp. poultry seasoning
Oil for cooking
6 Tbsp. flour
3 cups milk

SERVES 4

Pour ¼ inch oil in bottom of large skillet. Have it quite hot when you put the pieces of chicken in. Mix flour and seasonings in a plastic bag. Roll each piece of chicken in egg, then coat with seasoned flour. Fry on medium high heat—375° in electric skillet. When first side is golden brown, about 3 minutes, turn each piece. When this side is golden brown, 3-4 minutes, turn down heat, put lid on, leaving a small crack. Let chicken cook slowly for 10 more minutes before turning pieces again. Leave lid on, turning occasionally until the total cooking time from beginning is 40-45 minutes. Turn up heat for 2-4 minutes to crisp. Remove chicken from skillet and put onto platter in a 275-300° oven for 15 minutes while you make gravy and get dinner on the table.

To make gravy, pour out all but 3 tablespoons grease from skillet. Add 6 tablespoons of flour to grease and stir well to loosen chicken crumbs, making a paste. Add 3 cups milk gradually, stirring over medium high heat until desired consistency. Salt and pepper to taste. Serve with Baking Powder Biscuits (gravy on these is great), Country-Style Green Beans, mashed potatoes, and Chocolate Sheet Cake for dessert. Your family will ask for this meal again and again!

 Let cut up chicken soak in salt water overnight for a little extra flavor before frying it the next day.

CHICKEN DIVINE

2—10 oz. pkgs. frozen
  broccoli, cooked and
  drained
6 chicken breast halves,
  boiled and deboned
2 cans cream of chicken
  soup
1 cup mayonnaise
1 Tbsp. lemon juice
½ tsp. curry powder
1 cup grated cheddar
  cheese
Bread crumbs or potato
  chips

SERVES 6
Place cooked, drained broccoli in a greased shallow baking dish. Lay chicken on top of that. Combine soup, mayonnaise, lemon juice and curry powder. Pour over chicken and broccoli. Cover with grated cheese, then bread crumbs or crushed potato chips. Bake uncovered at 350° for 25-30 minutes.

JUDY'S WILD RICE CHICKEN

1 pkg. Uncle Ben's Wild
  Rice Mix
1 pkg. dry onion soup mix
1 can cream of mushroom
  soup
1¾ cup boiling water
¼ cup sherry
4 large chicken breast
  halves
Butter, melted
Salt, pepper to taste
Paprika

SERVES 4
Combine rice, soups, water and sherry in a 9 x 13 inch casserole. Place chicken breasts on top and brush with melted butter, salt, pepper and paprika. Cover and bake at 350° for 1½-2 hours.

CHICKEN & FISH

POTLUCK CHICKEN AND WILD RICE

1 large pkg. Uncle Ben's
   Instant Wild Rice
1 can cream of chicken
   soup
1 can cream of mushroom
   (or cream of celery) soup
2 cups milk
3 lbs. chicken, cut up

SERVES 4-6

Combine wild rice, soups, and milk in roasting pan. Mix well with spoon. Nestle the pieces of chicken into mixture. Cover and bake 1 hour 15 minutes at 350°. Check occasionally. Add more milk if rice begins to get dry. This really is a good potluck dish.

BIRDIE IN THE BAG

6 chicken breast halves
1 can cream of mushroom
   soup
½ cup dry white wine
1 Tbsp. green onion,
   chopped
Pinch of cayenne pepper
Salt and pepper to taste

SERVES 6

Tear off 6 squares of foil and place a chicken breast half on each square. In small saucepan, combine soup, wine, salt, pepper, green onion, and cayenne pepper. Heat and blend to a smooth sauce. Spoon sauce over each chicken breast and wrap securely. Set on cookie sheet and bake for 1 hour in 350° oven. Can be done in 9 x 13 inch casserole without wrapping individually. Cover tightly.

POTATO CHIP CHICKEN

2½ cups potato chips,
   crushed
¼ tsp. garlic salt
Dash of pepper
1 fryer, cut up
½ cup butter, melted

SERVES 4-6

Crush potato chips in plastic bag with a rolling pin. Add garlic salt and pepper to chips and shake well. Dip chicken in melted butter, then shake each piece in potato chips. Place in shallow baking dish, skin side up. Pour remaining butter and crumbs over chicken. Bake uncovered at 375° for 1 hour. Do not turn chicken. The flavor of fried chicken without the work!

CHICKEN CACCIATORE

¼ cup flour
½ tsp. salt
1—2½-3 lb. broiler-fryer
   chicken, cut up
¼ cup olive oil or salad oil
½ cup chopped onion
¼ cup chopped celery
¼ cup chopped green
   pepper
¼ tsp. garlic powder
1—16 oz. can tomatoes,
   cut up
1—8 oz. can tomato sauce
1—3 oz. can sliced
   mushrooms, drained
⅓ cup white wine
1 tsp. salt
½ tsp. dried basil leaves,
   crushed
½ tsp. dried rosemary
   leaves, crushed
Dash pepper

SERVES 4

Combine flour and ½ tsp. salt in plastic or paper bag; add a few pieces of chicken at a time and shake. In an ovenproof skillet, brown chicken in hot oil; remove chicken. In same skillet cook onion, celery, green pepper, and garlic until tender, but not brown. Return chicken to skillet. Combine tomatoes, tomato sauce, mushrooms, wine, salt, basil, rosemary, and pepper. Pour over chicken. Cover and bake at 350° until chicken is tender, about 1 hour. Remove the chicken to warm serving dish. Ladle sauce over top.

127

CHICKEN & FISH

CHICKEN SPAGHETTI

2 fryers, cut up
3 ribs celery, chopped
1 green pepper, chopped
2 onions, chopped
¼ tsp. garlic powder
1—4 oz. can sliced
  mushrooms, drained
1—10 oz. pkg. spaghetti,
  broken into ⅓'s or halves
1—1 lb. can tomatoes,
  chopped
2 Tbsp. ripe olives,
  chopped
1 can cream of mushroom
  soup
Salt and pepper
Paprika
Worcestershire sauce,
  several dashes
1 lb. Velveeta cheese,
  cubed

SERVES 10-12
Simmer chicken in salted water until tender. Remove chicken and all but 1 quart broth. Bone and dice chicken (you can tear the chicken into pieces and it's a lot less work). Set aside. Put celery, green pepper, onions, garlic powder and mushrooms into broth and cook several minutes. Add spaghetti and cook until it is done. Add remaining ingredients, and chicken, mixing well. Cook over low heat until cheese is melted. You can serve this right out of the Dutch oven immediately, or put it in a casserole and freeze for future use. Bake at 350° until it bubbles, about 30-45 minutes, if it has been frozen or refrigerated. Serve this easy one-pot meal with Spinach Salad, Cracked Wheat Bread, and Moist Coconut Cake. Everyone in your family (kids especially!) will love this meal.

CHICKEN ENCHILADAS

1 large fryer, cooked and
  boned
1 cup chopped onion
1 can cream of mushroom
  soup
1 can cream of chicken
  soup
½ cup chicken broth
2-3 Tbsp. green chilies,
  chopped (more if you
  like it hot)
1 dozen corn tortillas,
  torn into pieces
½ lb. cheddar cheese,
  grated

SERVES 8
Cook chicken in boiling, salted water until tender. Save stock. Debone chicken and cut into pieces. Mix onion, soups, broth, and green chilies in a bowl. Grease a 2 quart casserole and place a layer of tortilla pieces on the bottom. Add a layer of soup mixture, then chicken pieces, then grated cheese. Repeat this process one more time, ending with cheese. Bake at 350° uncovered for 45 minutes. Serve with Guacamole Salad and Sopapillas. Ole!

CHICKEN NOODLE CASSEROLE

3 cups (6 oz.) noodles
1 can condensed cream of
  chicken soup
⅓ cup sour cream
⅓ cup milk
1 Tbsp. chopped pimento
1 Tbsp. chopped parsley
⅓ cup chopped celery
Salt and pepper to taste
1 cup diced, cooked
  chicken
Buttered bread crumbs

SERVES 4-6
Cook noodles as package directs. Drain. Combine soup, sour cream, milk, pimento, parsley, celery and seasonings in saucepan. Heat thoroughly. Add chicken and noodles, mixing gently. Pour into greased 1½ quart casserole. Top with buttered bread crumbs. Bake uncovered in 375° oven 30 minutes. Good with tossed green salad, and Sourdough Bread.

CHICKEN AND DUMPLINGS

1 stewing chicken (4-5 lbs.)
  or 2 broiler-fryers (3 lbs.
  each)
1 small onion, sliced
2-3 carrots, sliced
3-4 ribs celery with leaves,
  chopped
1 tsp. salt
4 Tbsp. butter
6 Tbsp. flour
1/8 tsp. paprika
½ cup light cream
White pepper to taste

DUMPLINGS:
2 cups flour
1 tsp. salt
4 tsp. baking powder
1 Tbsp. shortening
¾ cup milk

SERVES 6-8
Simmer chicken, onion, carrots, celery and salt in enough water to cover. Cook until chicken is done, 1½-2 hours. Remove chicken from broth, saving 1 quart. When cool enough to handle, remove skin and bones, and dice meat. Melt butter in a cup. Stir in flour mixed with paprika. Add paste to chicken stock gradually, stirring constantly; cook for 2 minutes. Add chicken, cream, pepper, and adjust seasoning to taste. Spoon dumplings on top of gently bubbling chicken mixture and cover. Cook for 15 minutes without lifting lid. Serve at once.

To make dumplings, sift dry ingredients together. Blend in shortening with pastry blender or fork. Add milk and mix well. Dip teaspoon into cold water then into dough, and spoon dough onto chicken mixture as instructed. These are the best chicken and dumplings you will ever taste.

CHICKEN & FISH

EASY CHICKEN CHOW MEIN

1 chicken, cooked, deboned
  and cut up
1 quart chicken broth,
  reserved from stewed
  chicken
1 large can chow mein
  vegetables
1½ Tbsp. cornstarch
¼ cup water
1—10 oz. pkg. frozen
  Chinese snow peas
Chow Mein noodles
4 cups cooked rice
Soy Sauce

SERVES 4
Simmer chicken in salted water until tender. Remove chicken, debone, and cut into pieces. Reserve 1 quart of chicken broth. Add chicken and chow mein vegetables to broth. Mix cornstarch with ¼ cup water and add to chicken mixture. Add 1 tablespoon soy sauce and simmer 15-25 minutes. Add Chinese peas and simmer 5 more minutes. Serve over hot rice. Let each individual top serving with Chow Mein noodles and season with soy sauce.

HOT CHICKEN SALAD

2 cups cooked chicken
  (bite size)
2 cups chopped celery
½ cup slivered almonds
1 cup mayonnaise
1 cup crushed potato chips
½ cup grated cheddar
  cheese

SERVES 4
Mix the first four ingredients in a baking dish. Refrigerate several hours. Before cooking, cover with potato chips and cheese. Bake uncovered 20 minutes at 350°. This may be served as a cold chicken salad by eliminating the cheese and potato chips. Serve with Frosted Grapes, Croissants and Peach Melba for dessert. This is a light and refreshing summertime lunch.

Frosted Grapes: These are beautiful to look at and better to eat. Use them to garnish your poultry or ham dishes. Wash grapes and separate into small clusters. Beat 1 egg white in a small bowl until just broken up. Dip grapes into egg white. Let excess drip off. Dip grapes into superfine sugar to coat well. Place on a wire rack to dry.

CHICKEN AND BROCCOLI CREPES

4 Tbsp. butter
2 cups fresh mushrooms, sliced
6 Tbsp. flour
Dash salt
3 cups milk
½ cup sharp American cheese, shredded
¼ cup dry white wine
1—10 oz. pkg. frozen, chopped broccoli
2 cups finely chopped, cooked chicken
12-15 main dish crepes

12-15 CREPES
Sauce: In medium saucepan melt butter; saute mushrooms. Blend in flour and salt. Add milk all at once. Cook, stirring constantly, until thickened and bubbly. Stir in cheese and wine. Cook over low heat until cheese melts. Remove ½ cup of sauce; set aside.

Filling:
Cook broccoli according to package directions; drain. Combine drained broccoli, chicken, and ½ cup reserved sauce.

Spread rounded tablespoons of filling over unbrowned side of crepe, leaving ¼ inch rim around edge. Roll up crepe. Place, seam side down, in a skillet or chafing dish. Repeat with remaining crepes. Drizzle sauce over crepes. Cook, covered, over low heat until bubbly.

MAIN DISH CREPES:
1 cup flour
1½ cups milk
2 eggs
1 Tbsp. cooking oil
¼ tsp. salt

15 CREPES
In a bowl combine flour, milk, eggs, and salt; beat with mixer until blended. Heat a lightly greased 6-inch skillet. Remove from heat; spoon in about 2 tablespoons batter. Lift and tilt skillet to spread batter evenly. Return to heat; brown on one side only. (Cook on inverted crepe pan if you have one.) Invert pan and gently remove crepe with a fork. Repeat with remaining batter, greasing skillet occasionally.

CHICKEN & FISH

CHICKEN ROYALE

4 chicken breasts, deboned
¼ cup flour
½ tsp. salt
¼ tsp. paprika
Dash pepper

HERB STUFFING:
2 cups dry bread crumbs
1 Tbsp. chopped onion
½ tsp. salt
¼ tsp. poultry seasoning
Dash pepper
2 Tbsp. melted butter
¼ cup hot water
⅓ cup melted butter
Chopped parsley

MUSHROOM SAUCE:
½ lb. fresh mushrooms, sliced
¼ cup minced onion
2 Tbsp. butter
2 Tbsp. flour
½ cup cream
½ cup sour cream
½ tsp. salt
¼ tsp. pepper

SERVES 4
Combine flour and seasonings in bag, add chicken and shake. Combine bread crumbs, onion, ½ teaspoon salt, poultry seasoning, pepper, 2 tablespoons melted butter and hot water; mix well. Fill middle of chicken breast with stuffing. Roll together and secure with toothpick. Dip chicken in ⅓ cup melted butter, place in baking dish. Drizzle remaining butter over chicken. Bake uncovered at 325° for 45 minutes, turn, cover, and bake additional 45 minutes or until tender. Sprinkle with parsley and serve with Mushroom Sauce.

Sauce: Cook mushrooms and onions lightly in butter until tender. Push mushrooms to one side and stir flour into butter. Add cream, sour cream and seasonings. Heat slowly, stirring constantly, almost to boiling point. Spoon over hot chicken.

Try serving this with Stir-Fried Broccoli and Carrots, Orange Rolls and Cheese Cake. Goodness in every bite!

CHRIS'S CRAB-STUFFED CHICKEN

**8 chicken breast halves,
   boned and skinned**
4 Tbsp. margarine
¼ cup flour
¾ cup milk
¾ cup chicken bouillon
⅓ cup white wine
¼ cup onion, chopped
**7½ oz. can crab, drained
   and flaked**
**3 oz. can chopped
   mushrooms, drained**
½ cup bread crumbs
2 Tbsp. parsley, chopped
½ tsp. salt
Dash of pepper
½ tsp. paprika
**½ cup Swiss cheese,
   grated**

SERVES 8

Place a chicken breast half between 2 pieces of waxed paper and, working from the center, pound the chicken lightly to make it approximately 1/8 inch thick and 8 x 3 inches. Repeat with each piece of chicken and set aside. In a small saucepan, melt 3 tablespoons margarine and blend in flour, then add milk gradually. Add chicken bouillon and wine all at once. Cook until it thickens and bubbles. Set aside. Cook onion in 1 tablespoon margarine until tender, but not brown. Stir in crabmeat, mushrooms, bread crumbs, parsley, salt, and pepper. Stir in ½ cup sauce. Top each chicken piece with the crab mixture, fold in sides and roll up; secure with toothpick. Place seam side down in a large baking dish. Pour balance of sauce over all and bake covered in 350° oven for 1 hour. Uncover and sprinkle with cheese and paprika. Return to oven until cheese melts, about 10 minutes. This is a special occasion dish that will impress your guests. Serve with Rich Green Salad, Whole Wheat Bread, and Chocolate Marengo.

 Parsley can be frozen—when you buy a fresh bunch, wash it, trim the stems and dry in a towel. Roll it up in foil and put it in the freezer. When you need chopped parsley, remove it from the freezer and grate it. No chopping board is necessary. Grate the amount you need and return the rest to the freezer.

CHICKEN AND DRESSING CASSEROLE

1—8 oz. pkg. Pepperidge
    Farm Herb Seasoned
    Stuffing Mix
1 stick margarine, melted
1 cup water
2½ cups cooked diced
    chicken
½ cup chopped onions
¼ cup green onion tops or
    chives
½ cup celery, chopped
½ cup mayonnaise
¾ tsp. salt
2 eggs, slightly beaten
1½ cups milk
1 can cream of mushroom
    soup, undiluted
1 cup cheddar cheese,
    grated

SERVES 8
Combine stuffing mix, butter, and water; toss lightly. Put half of mixture in buttered 9 x 12 inch shallow casserole. Mix together the chicken, onions, chives, celery, mayonnaise, and salt. Spoon over the stuffing mixture. Mix beaten eggs and milk, pour evenly over chicken and stuffing. Cover with foil and refrigerate overnight. One hour before baking, take out of refrigerator and spread cream of mushroom soup over top. Bake uncovered 40 minutes at 325°. Sprinkle grated cheese over top and return to oven for 10 minutes. Serve with Hot Curried Fruit, Orange Rolls, and Dessert Delight for a rich meal. Freezes well.

CORNISH GAME HENS

4 Cornish game hens
¼ cup flour
Salt
Pepper
Pinch of nutmeg
1 tsp. paprika
¼ lb. butter
6 slices onion
1/8 tsp. garlic powder
½ bay leaf
Pinch of thyme
1 can sliced mushrooms
2 slices bacon
2 cups burgundy

SERVES 4
Wipe thawed hens dry. Coat hens in ¼ cup flour, seasoned with salt, pepper, nutmeg and paprika. Melt 2 tablespoons of the butter in a large skillet, and brown hens. Remove and put in a roasting pan. In skillet combine remaining butter, 6 slices of onion, garlic, bay leaf, thyme, and can of sliced mushrooms. Simmer 10 minutes. Pour butter-onion mixture over hens, cover each with bacon; then pour burgundy over hens. Cover and cook at 250° about 2½ hours or more. Serve with Spinach Salad and wild rice.

OLD FASHIONED CHICKEN & NOODLES

1 large chicken
Salt and pepper
2 chicken bouillon cubes

NOODLES:
2½ cups flour
2 eggs
6 Tbsp. butter
½ tsp. salt
1 tsp. cream of tartar
¾ cup whipping cream

SERVES 6

Cook chicken in 2½ quarts of water. Season with salt and pepper. When tender, debone and cut meat into pieces. Save broth.

Combine flour, eggs, salt and cream of tartar in bowl. Work ingredients with fingers to mix well. Gradually add cream. Continue working dough, adding only enough cream to make a very dry dough that will gather together. Flour a large cutting board or countertop generously. Roll noodle dough very thin, about 1/8 inch or less. Dust flour over top if sticky. Dough needs to be very dry and flour can be worked in with rolling pin. Roll up dough jelly roll style and slice off noodles about 1/8 inch thick. The noodle rolls should easily shake out. If not, the dough is still too sticky. These noodles don't need to dry, but do dry well if you want to make them ahead of time. Add noodles to 1¾-2 quarts of boiling chicken broth. Add 2 chicken bouillon cubes and let noodles simmer 15 minutes, or until done, before adding chicken. Add chicken, salt and pepper to taste. Chicken and noodles are an all time favorite . . . sure to become a regular in your menu planning. For a variation, substitute beef for the chicken to make hearty beef and noodles.

Throw several ice cubes into meat or chicken broth that has grease to be removed. The grease will stick to the cubes.

CHICKEN & FISH

CHICKEN, QUAIL OR PHEASANT IN CREAM SAUCE

Flour, seasoned with salt, pepper, and poultry seasoning
2½ lb. chicken, quail or pheasant, cut into serving size pieces
6 Tbsp. butter
½ lb. mushrooms, sliced
¼ cup almonds, sliced
½ onion, chopped
3 stalks celery, chopped
1 pint cream
1 tsp. salt
¼ tsp. pepper
½ cup dry sherry

SERVES 4
Put flour and seasonings in bag. Shake pieces of meat in flour to coat. Brown in 4 tablespoons melted butter. Remove pieces from skillet to casserole dish. In skillet, saute mushrooms, almonds, onion, and celery in 2 tablespoons butter until tender. Pour sauteed mixture over meat. Cover and bake at 350° for 30 minutes. Mix together cream, salt, pepper, and sherry; add to meat. Cover and bake 45 additional minutes or until birds are tender.

ORANGE-BAKED PHEASANT BREASTS

4 pheasant breasts
⅓ cup flour
1 tsp. salt
1/8 tsp. pepper
½ cup cooking oil
½ tsp. celery seed
1 thinly sliced onion
1 cup fresh orange juice
1 cup water
½ unpeeled orange, cut in wedges

SERVES 4
Wash and dry pheasant breasts. Combine flour, salt and pepper and coat breasts with flour mixture. Heat oil in heavy skillet; add pheasant; sprinkle with celery seed. Brown both sides over low heat. Remove pheasant from skillet and place in 2 quart baking dish. Cook onion in same skillet until tender. Add orange juice and water, and bring to boil. Pour over pheasant. Arrange orange wedges over pheasant. Cover and bake in 300° oven for 1 hour. Reduce heat to 250° and bake an additional hour. Delicious with Chicken Rice-a-Roni or Uncle Ben's Wild Rice.

SUSIE'S ROMERTOFF WILD DUCK

1 wild duck, cleaned
½ tsp. salt
¼ tsp. pepper
¼ tsp. garlic powder
½ onion, quartered
½ apple, quartered
1 orange, quartered
3 or 4 cinnamon sticks

SERVES 4

Wash and clean wild duck. Sprinkle with salt, pepper and garlic. Place onion, apple and orange in cavity of duck. Soak Romertoff pot for 15 minutes in a sink full of water. Place duck on sticks of cinnamon in pot and bake at 250-300° for 2 hours. Do not preheat oven. Occasionally baste the duck. Serve with Uncle Ben's Wild Rice. If you do not have a Romertoff cooker (a clay pot cooker), you can use a regular roaster, but add 2-3 cups water.

JOHNNY APPLESEED TURKEY STUFFING

1 stick butter or margarine
1 small onion, chopped
1 cup celery, chopped
2 apples, peeled, cored and chopped
1—10 oz. can chicken broth
1—8 oz. pkg. Pepperidge Farm Herb Seasoned Stuffing
4 slices bacon, crisply fried and crumbled

MAKES ENOUGH TO STUFF AN 8-10 LB. TURKEY

Melt butter. Add onion and celery. Saute until onion is transparent. Add apples and broth. Heat to boiling point. Combine apple mixture with stuffing mix and bacon. Mix well. Just before turkey is ready to be roasted, spoon stuffing in body and neck cavities. This can also be served hot from the saucepan or casserole dish.

Hot applesauce complements all game.

CHICKEN & FISH

MARY'S SCALLOPED OYSTERS

1 lb. butter
1 lb. saltine crackers (more or less)
4 cans Geisha whole oysters
1 can water chestnuts, sliced
Milk to cover
Parsley
Nutmeg
Salt
Pepper

SERVES 12-15
Melt butter and add coarsely crumbled crackers. Toss well. Spread a layer in large casserole. Cover with 1½ cans oysters, oyster liquid, ⅓ can water chestnuts. Season with salt, pepper, nutmeg, and parsley. Continue layering until all oysters and water chestnuts are used. Top with buttered crumbs and parsley. Just before heating, add milk to within one inch of crumb top. Cook uncovered at 400° for ½ hour. This is an unusually delicious and easy recipe. The oyster dish will add a gala look and zesty flavor to beef, pork or lamb.

CREAMED SCALLOPS AND MUSHROOMS

1 lb. fresh or frozen scallops
2 Tbsp. butter
1 cup fresh mushrooms, sliced
¼ cup margarine
¼ cup flour
½ tsp. salt
¼ tsp. pepper
½ cup water
1½ cups half and half
½ cup cheddar cheese, grated
2 Tbsp. fresh parsley
Paprika

SERVES 4
Thaw, rinse and wipe scallops dry. Saute mushrooms in butter. Set aside. Grease shallow casserole and arrange scallops in bottom. In small saucepan, melt margarine and stir in flour, salt, and pepper until blended. Gradually add half and half, stirring constantly. Add mushrooms and water. Cook, stirring constantly, until thick and smooth. Stir in parsley and pour over scallops. Sprinkle with cheese and paprika on top. Bake uncovered at 350° for 30 minutes or until cheese melts and sauce is bubbly. Serve over rice or toasted patty shells.

DODIE'S CURRIED SCALLOPS

2 lbs. scallops
Seasoned flour (with salt
    and pepper)
8 Tbsp. butter
6 green onions, finely diced
1½ Tbsp. curry powder
⅓ cup dry white wine
5 cups cooked rice

SERVES 4-6
Wash and dry scallops. Dust lightly with seasoned flour. Heat butter in skillet and saute green onions for 3 minutes. Add scallops and cook quickly, turning frequently to brown, about 3 minutes. Sprinkle with curry powder. Add wine and mix well. Serve immediately over rice.

SEAFOOD LUNCHEON DISH

1 can cream of mushroom
    soup
⅔ cup milk
¼ cup cheese, grated
    (Longhorn)
½ cup mayonnaise
2 cups fine noodles,
    crushed slightly
2 cups cooked shrimp
1—6½ oz. can crabmeat,
    drained
1—5 oz. can water
    chestnuts, drained
1 can French fried onion
    rings, crushed

SERVES 6
Mix soup, milk, cheese, and mayonnaise. Fold in uncooked noodles, shrimp, crab, and sliced water chestnuts. Pour into greased 2 quart casserole. Bake, covered, at 325° for 20 minutes. Uncover and bake an additional 10 minutes. Sprinkle with onion rings and bake 10 minutes longer or until noodles are tender. Serve with Banana-Berry Gelatin Salad, Raisin Bran Muffins and Peggy's Lemon Bars.

CHICKEN & FISH

FISH FRY

Trout, catfish, snapper,
   whitefish, oysters,
   scallops, bass
Cornmeal
Vegetable oil for frying
Lemon juice
Paprika
Dry mustard
Salt and pepper

Skin and fillet fish; cut into strips. Soak fish in lemon juice 5 minutes. Season fish lightly with salt and paprika. Drop fish strips into a bag with cornmeal which has been seasoned with salt, pepper, and dry mustard. Fry fish in hot oil until golden. Serve with ketchup, Tabasco, Hush Puppies, and Cole Slaw. This meal will send the fishermen in your family back for more!

BARBECUED FISH

Scallops, whole fresh
   shrimp, halibut or salmon
Butter
Fresh lemon juice
Salt
Parsley

Baste fish with melted butter mixed with lemon juice, salt and parsley as it cooks on barbecuer. Kabobs can be made using whole scallops, shrimp, and/or chunks of other fish fillets, along with onion pieces, mushrooms, and tomato wedges. A delicious and easy way to fix your favorite fish.

SALMON CROQUETS

1—7¾ oz. can salmon
   drained
5 saltine crackers, crushed
2 eggs, slightly beaten
⅓ onion, chopped
1 tsp. salt
Pepper

SERVES 4
Combine all ingredients in bowl. Form into patties. Fry slowly in butter, turning once, about 7 minutes on each side. Delicious served with Pan Fried Potatoes and Corn Cheese Bake.

■▼■▼■▼■▼■▼■▼■▼■▼■▼■▼■▼■▼■▼■▼■▼■▼■

SHRIMP AND GREEN NOODLE CASSEROLE

¼ lb. mushrooms, sliced
2 Tbsp. butter
1—12 oz. pkg. green
   noodles
2 cans cream of mushroom
   soup
1½ lb. shrimp, cooked
2 tsp. curry powder
¼ tsp. oregano
¼ tsp. paprika
1 cup sour cream
½ cup sherry
½ cup sauterne (wine)
Wheat germ

SERVES 12
Saute mushrooms in butter. Cook green noodles according to package directions. Drain. Combine remaining ingredients and put into greased 2 quart casserole. Bake 45 minutes at 350°. Sprinkle top with wheat germ and return to oven for 5 minutes.

BAKED TROUT

4 small trout, cleaned,
   washed and dried
4 sprigs fresh (or ½ tsp.
   dried) thyme
Juice of 1 lemon
4 thin slices bacon
4 sheets of aluminum foil
4 Tbsp. butter

SERVES 4
Preheat oven to 400°. Place a sprig of fresh thyme inside each trout. Sprinkle with lemon juice; then wrap each trout in a slice of bacon. Grease each sheet of foil with a quarter of the butter. Completely enclose the fish in foil. Place packets on a baking dish and bake for 10 minutes. Lower temperature to 350° and bake for an additional 10 minutes. Serve trout in their foil packages.

COLORADO TROUT

½ lb. bacon
1 large onion, sliced
2-3 fresh, pan-sized trout
½ cup cornmeal
½ cup flour
1½ tsp. salt
Pepper

SERVES 2
Fry and drain bacon. Saute onion in bacon fat. Set onions on plate with bacon. Roll trout in seasoned cornmeal and flour mixture. Fry in hot bacon fat. When trout is almost done, about 10 minutes, top with bacon and onion. Put lid on pan and leave on low heat for 5-10 minutes. This can be done easily at campsite!

Vegetables,

Rice

&

Pasta

VEGETABLES, RICE & PASTA

MARY'S BAKED BEANS

4—16 oz. Campbell's Old
   Fashioned or Homestyle
   Beans
1 green pepper, chopped
1 medium onion, chopped
2 strips uncooked bacon,
   cut in 1 inch pieces
¼ cup brown sugar
1 Tbsp. Poupon mustard

SERVES 10
Mix all ingredients and bake uncovered at 325° for 2 hours.

COWBOY BEANS

2 cups pinto beans, washed
   well
1½ tsp. salt
¼ cup bacon drippings
2-3 tsp. chili powder
¼ tsp. pepper
Cold water to cover
   (about 1-1½ qts.)

SERVES 8
Put all ingredients in large Dutch oven
or crock pot. Simmer 6-8 hours or
until beans are tender. If cooking in
crock pot, cook on high. To thicken
juice, spoon out about ½ cup beans,
mash with a fork, and return to pot.
These are easiest of all to cook in a
pressure cooker. Set weight at 15
lbs., and cook for 2 hours. These
beans are great with fried chicken,
barbecue, steak, ham, or for Mexican
food fixin's. They freeze well.

VEGETABLES, RICE & PASTA

COUNTRY STYLE GREEN BEANS

1—16 oz. bag frozen green
   beans or fresh green
   beans
¾ cup ham or bacon,
   cut-up
1 Tbsp. instant diced
   onions
1 Tbsp. bacon fat
2½ tsp. salt
6-8 small new potatoes,
   washed and unpeeled
   (optional)

SERVES 6

Cover beans with water in large saucepan. Add other ingredients. Cover with lid and boil for 10 minutes. Remove lid and simmer for 2 hours or until water is cooked down to about 1-2 inches. Remove from heat, cover with lid, and let sit a couple hours, to blend flavors. Before serving, cook 15 more minutes. It's best to let beans cook until most of liquid is gone. Don't let them cook dry and burn. This is also good with new potatoes. If using new potatoes, the peelings can be left on, and cooked whole with beans.

EPICUREAN GREEN BEANS

1 lb. fresh green beans,
   cut into 1 inch pieces,
   or 2—1 lb. cans green
   beans
1 cup fresh mushrooms,
   sliced
1 Tbsp. chopped onion
2 Tbsp. butter
3 Tbsp. flour
Dash pepper
½ tsp. salt
¼ tsp. thyme
2 cups milk
4 slices bacon, cooked
   and crumbled
1—10 oz. pkg. frozen patty
   shells, baked (optional)

SERVES 6

Cook beans in boiling, salted water until tender, about 15 minutes. In 2 quart saucepan, cook mushrooms and onion in butter until tender. Blend in flour, salt, thyme, and pepper. Add milk all at once. Cook, stirring constantly until mixture thickens and bubbles. Stir in beans, heat through. Add bacon. Spoon mixture into prepared patty shells. If desired, garnish with additional crumbled bacon.

VEGETABLES, RICE & PASTA

BUTTERY ITALIAN GREEN BEANS

2—9 oz. pkg. frozen
Italian green beans
1½ cups fresh mushrooms,
sliced
6 Tbsp. butter
½ tsp. salt

SERVES 4-6

Cook green beans in boiling salted water for 5 minutes. Drain well. Melt butter in large skillet, saute mushrooms. Add beans to mushrooms in skillet. Sprinkle with salt. Stir and let simmer 5 minutes. Cover with lid and remove from heat until serving time. Before serving, heat thoroughly again. (Better if made ½-1 hour ahead of serving, to allow mushroom and bean flavors to blend.)

SWEET AND SOUR BEANS

1—15 oz. can white lima
beans, drained
1—15 oz. can green lima
beans, drained
1—15 oz. can kidney
beans, drained
1 large can Pork and
Beans
1½ medium onions, sliced
or chopped
1 scant cup brown sugar
1 Tbsp. dry mustard
½ cup vinegar
1 tsp. garlic salt
1 tsp. salt
4 slices of bacon,
chopped

SERVES 12

Combine all ingredients except bacon in large casserole. Mix well and top with chopped bacon. Bake uncovered 2-2½ hours at 350°.

Sprinkle a burnt pan generously with baking soda, dampen slightly, set aside for a few days and rinse.

VEGETABLES, RICE & PASTA

GRANDMOTHER'S ISLAND BEAN CASSEROLE

2—1 lb. cans Blue Lake
  whole green beans
  (save juice)
1 Tbsp. bacon drippings
1½ tsp. dill seed

SAUCE:
6 Tbsp. flour
6 Tbsp. butter, melted
1 cup bean juice
1 cup milk
3 Tbsp. grated onion
1 tsp. black pepper
2½ tsp. mei yen (Spice
  Island)
Bread crumbs or slivered
  almonds

SERVES 6-8
Simmer green beans, drippings, and dill seed at a low temperature for 30 minutes. Make sauce by stirring flour into melted butter, then gradually adding liquids, stirring constantly. Add seasonings, stir well. Stir green beans into sauce, mix and put in casserole dish. Sprinkle bread crumbs or slivered almonds on top. Bake uncovered 20 minutes, or until bubbly, at 350°.

GREEN BEAN CASSEROLE

¼ cup butter
⅓ cup onion, chopped
½ lb. mushrooms, sliced
1—5 oz. can water
  chestnuts, sliced
⅓ cup flour
1 tsp. soy sauce
1/8 tsp. Tabasco
1/8 tsp. salt
1½ cups milk
1 cup cheddar cheese,
  grated
2 or 3—1 lb. cans
  green beans
1 small can French fried
  onion rings
Dash pepper

SERVES 6-8
Melt ¼ cup butter in skillet. Saute onion and mushrooms. Blend in flour; add milk, soy sauce, Tabasco, salt and pepper. Stir over medium heat until smooth. Add cheese and continue cooking until melted. Add onions, mushrooms, and water chestnuts to sauce. Mix well. Drain green beans; place in buttered casserole. Pour sauce over beans and mix. Bake uncovered at 350° for 45 minutes. Arrange onion rings on top and bake additional 10 minutes.

GREEN BEANS CAESAR

1½ lbs. fresh green beans
    (or 2—1 lb. cans green
    beans, heated through; or
    2—9 oz. pkg. frozen cut
    green beans, cooked and
    drained)
2 Tbsp. salad oil
1 Tbsp. vinegar
1 Tbsp. instant minced
    onion
¼ tsp. salt
1/8 tsp. garlic powder
1/8 tsp. pepper
2 Tbsp. dry bread crumbs
2 Tbsp. grated Parmesan
    cheese
1 Tbsp. butter or
    margarine, melted
Paprika

SERVES 6

Place fresh beans cut in pieces, in 1 inch salted water. Cook uncovered until tender, about 10 minutes. Drain well. Heat oven to 350°. Toss beans with oil, vinegar, onion, salt, garlic and pepper. Pour into 1 quart casserole. Stir together crumbs, cheese and butter. Sprinkle over beans. Garnish with paprika. Bake uncovered 15-20 minutes.

ALMOND-BROCCOLI CASSEROLE

2—10 oz. pkg. frozen
    broccoli stalks
1—8 oz. can small whole
    onions, drain and reserve
    juice
1 Tbsp. lemon juice
2 Tbsp. butter
2 Tbsp. flour
1 Tbsp. sugar
½ tsp. salt
1 cup milk
½ cup grated Parmesan
    cheese
1/8 cup white wine
1/8 cup juice from onions
½ cup toasted slivered
    almonds

SERVES 6-8

Cook broccoli in boiling salted water 8 minutes, drain. Arrange broccoli and onions in bottom of buttered casserole and sprinkle with lemon juice. Melt butter in saucepan, stir in flour; add milk, sugar, and salt. Stir until thick and smooth. Blend in Parmesan cheese, wine and onion juice. Pour over broccoli and onions. Sprinkle with toasted almonds. (To toast: arrange almonds in pie plate in 350° oven, shake occasionally, toast to golden brown.) Bake uncovered at 350° for 25 minutes.

VEGETABLES, RICE & PASTA

STIR-FRIED BROCCOLI AND CARROTS

2 Tbsp. oil
1/8 tsp. garlic powder
½ cup broccoli flowerets
1 cup carrots, sliced thin
1 small onion, cut into rings
¾ cup chicken broth
1 tsp. seasoning salt
1 Tbsp. cornstarch
1 Tbsp. cold water
1 can water chestnuts,
   drained
1 cup sliced mushrooms

SERVES 6
Heat oil, add garlic, broccoli, carrots, and onion; stir fry 1 minute. Add broth and seasoned salt, cover and cook about 3 minutes. Mix cornstarch and water, stir into vegetables. Cook and stir until thickened, about 10 seconds. Add water chestnuts and mushrooms. Cook and stir 30 seconds.

BROCCOLI-CAULIFLOWER CASSEROLE

2—10 oz. pkg. frozen
   broccoli stalks
1—10 oz. pkg. frozen
   cauliflower
2 Tbsp. flour
2 Tbsp. butter
1½ cups milk
1 cup Velveeta cheese,
   diced
Dash pepper
½ tsp. salt
1—4 oz. can mushrooms,
   or ¾ cup fresh
   mushrooms
¼ cup butter
2 cups bread crumbs

SERVES 8
Cook broccoli and cauliflower according to package directions, drain well. Melt butter in saucepan, add flour and stir to make a paste. Gradually add milk, stirring constantly. When sauce is thick and smooth, add Velveeta, salt, pepper, and mushrooms. (If using fresh mushrooms, saute in 1 tablespoon butter.) Arrange broccoli and cauliflower in bottom of buttered casserole and cover with cheese sauce. Melt ¼ cup butter in skillet, add bread crumbs, and stir over low heat for 5 minutes. Sprinkle over casserole. Bake uncovered at 350° for 20 minutes or until hot throughout.

BROCCOLI WITH WALNUTS

3—10 oz. pkg. frozen chopped broccoli, cooked and drained
1 stick butter or margarine, melted
¼ cup flour
1½ Tbsp. instant chicken broth granules
2 cups milk
⅔ cup hot water
6 Tbsp. butter or margarine
2 cups Pepperidge Farm stuffing mix
⅔ cup chopped walnuts

SERVES 8

Arrange cooked broccoli in buttered 9 x 13 inch casserole dish. Melt one stick of butter in small saucepan. Add flour and broth granules. Cook a few minutes, stirring constantly. Add milk gradually and stir until smooth and thick. Pour this sauce over broccoli. Melt 6 tablespoons butter in hot water; add stuffing mix and toss thoroughly. Add walnuts and mix. Spoon on top of broccoli and bake uncovered in a 400° oven about 30 minutes. This freezes well. This will be the best broccoli casserole you'll ever taste.

CREAMED CABBAGE

½ head cabbage, sliced
½ small onion, sliced
¼ cup water
Salt and pepper
½ cup cream
1 Tbsp. sugar
1 tsp. cornstarch

SERVES 4

Cover cabbage and onion with water in saucepan. Cook until tender. Drain water. Add cream, sugar, salt and pepper to cabbage. Mix cornstarch with ¼ cup water and add to cabbage. Bring to bubbly stage stirring constantly. Reduce heat and serve.

 When cooking cabbage add a stalk of celery to prevent odor.

CORN CHEESE BAKE

1—3 oz. pkg. cream
   cheese, softened
¼ cup milk
1 Tbsp. butter or margarine
½ tsp. onion salt
1—1 lb. can whole kernel
   corn, drained (or 1—10
   oz. pkg. frozen corn,
   cooked and drained)
Paprika

SERVES 4-5
Combine cream cheese, milk, butter and onion salt in saucepan; stir over low heat until cheese melts. Stir corn into cheese. Pour into small casserole. Sprinkle with paprika. Cook uncovered until bubbly, about 10 minutes, in a 350° oven. Good with Prime Rib or steaks.

CORN PUDDING

2—10 oz. pkg. frozen corn
2 Tbsp. chives
1 Tbsp. sugar
1 tsp. salt
1 tsp. pepper
2 large eggs, beaten
1½ cups whipping cream

SERVES 6-8
Mix all ingredients in 2 quart casserole dish. Cover and bake at 250° for 3-4 hours.

CREAMY EGGPLANT

1 eggplant, peeled and cut
   into chunks
3 Tbsp. butter, melted
⅓ cup cracker crumbs
1 cup cream
¼ cup cheddar cheese,
   grated
2 Tbsp. Parmesan cheese

SERVES 4
Boil eggplant in water 10-15 minutes or until tender. Drain. Add cracker crumbs and melted butter. Arrange in bottom of buttered casserole dish. Pour cream over top and sprinkle with cheeses. Bake uncovered at 350° for 25 minutes or until bubbly throughout.

 Add sugar and a little lemon juice, not salt, to the cooking water for corn on the cob. Salt will toughen it.

VEGETABLES, RICE & PASTA

MARINAN'S GARLIC-CHEESE GRITS

6 cups boiling water
1½ cups grits
1½ sticks butter
1½ cups (1 lb.) grated
American cheese
3 eggs, beaten
1½ tsp. salt
4-6 shakes Tabasco
¼ tsp. minced garlic

SERVES 10
Add grits to boiling water. Reduce heat; simmer 5 minutes stirring constantly. Combine with other ingredients and mix well. Bake uncovered in large buttered bowl for 1 hour 15 minutes at 325°. Good at breakfast with scrambled eggs, hot biscuits and gravy, or at other meals as a potato substitute.

BEST-EVER GREENS

Large saucepan full of
fresh greens (turnip,
collard, spinach),
chopped or whole
2 Tbsp. bacon fat
2-3 pieces bacon, sliced
into small pieces
1½ tsp. salt

SERVES 4
Pour 1 inch of water in bottom of saucepan. Add greens, fat, bacon and salt. Let simmer, covered, until greens cook down, about 10 minutes. Uncover and let simmer 45 minutes-1 hour. Stir occasionally, making sure they don't cook dry. Let sit in covered pan 2-6 hours for extra flavor . . . the longer, the better. Before serving, cook additional 15 minutes. Eat with vinegar sprinkled on top or with salt and butter.

DORIS' HOMINEY CASSEROLE

1 large can hominey
(1 lb. 13 oz.)
1 cup sour cream
1—7 oz. can green chilies,
chopped
1 tsp. salt
1 cup grated cheddar
cheese

SERVES 4
Combine hominey, sour cream, chilies and salt. Mix well. Cover with grated cheddar cheese. Bake uncovered at 350° until hot and cheese is melted, about 25-30 minutes.

VEGETABLES, RICE & PASTA

COUNTRY FRIED MUSHROOMS

1 lb. fresh mushrooms
3 eggs
1-1½ cups flour
⅓ cup butter
Salt and pepper

SERVES 4-6
Wash mushrooms. Gently pull stems from caps. Save and use them, too! Let sit on towel to dry, or dab excess moisture off. Beat eggs in small bowl. Dip mushrooms and stems in egg, roll in flour. Fry slowly in melted butter, stirring gently. Salt and pepper to taste. After browning on both sides, put lid on loosely and turn down heat. Cook until mushrooms are done— about 20 minutes. These can also be served as the main course as they are very filling.

OKRA AND TOMATOES

2 lbs. okra, washed and
  sliced (tips and stem
  ends removed)
2 cups water
1 medium onion, sliced
1 Tbsp. vinegar
1½ tsp. salt
2 Tbsp. bacon drippings
1—16 oz. can stewed
  tomatoes
½ tsp. sugar
1/8 tsp. pepper

SERVES 6-8
Combine okra, water, onion, vinegar, and 1½ tsp. salt. Cover and cook over medium high heat for 15 minutes. Drain; cook, uncovered, over low heat until all moisture evaporates. Add remaining ingredients; cook over medium heat, turning frequently, 5 minutes.

Try using milk in place of water when cooking peas, limas, or spinach. Adds flavor and nutrition.

VEGETABLES, RICE & PASTA

WEST TEXAS FRIED OKRA

1 lb. okra, sliced with
   stems and tips removed
1 cup cornmeal
Bacon drippings
Salt

SERVES 4
Pour cornmeal in a plastic bag, add okra and shake. Cook okra in bacon drippings stirring over medium high heat until golden brown. Salt well. Drain on paper towel. Serve hot. When okra is prepared this way, it is crunchy and light . . . a real taste treat!

MOM'S ONION RINGS

1 cup flour
¼ tsp. salt
½ cup (small can)
   evaporated milk
2 Tbsp. salad oil
1 egg white
6 Tbsp. water
2-3 large onions (Bermuda
   onions work best)

SERVES 4
Combine all ingredients except onions. Mix well with beater. Slice onions and take rings apart. Dip in batter and deep fry at 375°, turning once, until golden brown. Sprinkle with salt. Place in warm oven until ready to serve. These never fail!

SOUTHERN STYLE BLACK-EYED PEAS

2 lbs. fresh black-eyed
   peas, washed and
   podded (young tender
   ones can just be
   snapped)
Salt pork, sliced (or ¼ cup
   bacon drippings)
Salt and pepper to taste

SERVES 8
Cover peas with water, add salt pork, salt and pepper. Cook over low heat for 2-3 hours. These are better the second day. It has been a tradition for as long as can be remembered to serve black-eyed peas on New Year's Day as a measure of good luck. It's also fun to hide a thoroughly washed dime in the peas and whoever gets the dime in their portion will become rich in the New Year.

154

VEGETABLES, RICE & PASTA

CREAMED PEAS

1—16 oz. pkg. frozen peas,
   or 3 cups fresh peas
4 Tbsp. butter
2 Tbsp. flour
1 cup half and half
Heaping tsp. sugar
½ tsp. salt

SERVES 6-8
Cook peas in boiling water for 10 minutes. Pour into colander and drain. Using same saucepan, melt butter over medium heat and stir in flour. Gradually add half and half, stirring constantly until thick and creamy. Stir in sugar, salt and peas. If adding carrots, cook 1 cup sliced carrots until tender in separate saucepan. Add to creamed peas.

COUNTRY POTATOES

12 red or new potatoes
   (baking potatoes can be
   substituted)
6 strips cooked bacon,
   crumbled
2 cups sharp cheddar
   cheese, grated
½ stick butter, melted
Salt and pepper to taste

SERVES 8
Boil potatoes, with skins on, until done. Drain and let cool. Thinly slice the unpeeled potatoes. Butter bottom of 9 x 12 inch baking dish. Put one layer of potatoes, salt, pepper, half of cheese and bacon in casserole. Dribble half of the butter over layer. Make another layer the same way. Bake uncovered at 350° until bubbling hot, about 15 minutes. This potato recipe is guaranteed to please! Freezes well.

SOUR CREAM POTATOES

8-10 medium potatoes,
   pared, cooked and
   mashed
8 oz. cream cheese
¼-½ cup sour cream
Butter
Paprika

SERVES 8
Whip cheese and sour cream until light. Gradually add mashed potatoes to cheese mixture. Top with butter and paprika. Cook 20-25 minutes at 325°. This may be frozen and reheated.

VEGETABLES, RICE & PASTA

SARAH LEW'S LAYERED POTATO CASSEROLE

4 medium raw potatoes,
  pared and sliced
½ head cabbage, sliced
1½ cups apple, diced
1 medium onion, sliced
Salt and pepper
3 Tbsp. butter
½ pint whipping cream
½ cup Parmesan cheese
¾ cup bread crumbs

SERVES 8
Butter a 3 quart, long, flat casserole. Begin with potatoes as the bottom layer, and layer the cabbage, apple and onion. Place butter dabs on top; pour whipping cream evenly over casserole. Bake 45 minutes at 350°, covered. Uncover and top with Parmesan cheese and bread crumbs; brown an additional 10-15 minutes.

SWEET POTATO CASSEROLE

1 large can sweet
  potatoes
¾ stick margarine or
  butter, melted
1¼ cups sugar
½ tsp. cinnamon
½ tsp. nutmeg
2 eggs

TOPPING:
¾ cup corn flake crumbs
½ cup chopped nuts
½ cup brown sugar
¾ stick melted margarine

SERVES 4-6
Warm potatoes and syrup, and mash to a very smooth consistency. Use a blender, food processor or mixer to do this. Add other ingredients; mix well. Place in 2 quart casserole dish. Bake uncovered 20 minutes at 400°. Spread topping, which has been mixed together, on potatoes and brown for another 10 minutes.

VEGETABLES, RICE & PASTA

PAN FRIED POTATOES

1 Tbsp. butter
1 Tbsp. Crisco
5 medium potatoes, sliced
   ¼ inch thick
1½ tsp. salt
Pepper
¼-½ purple onion, sliced

SERVES 4
Melt butter and shortening in skillet. Let oil get fairly hot (300°). Add potato slices. Sprinkle with half the salt. Let fry 10 minutes at medium high heat, turning to get most of them browned. Season with remaining salt. Slice onion over potatoes, cover with lid. Let simmer over low heat, 275°, for 15 minutes, stirring occasionally until potatoes are tender. Before serving, turn up heat and remove lid to crisp. Good with Chicken Fried Steak and Cream Gravy.

FAVORITE HASHED BROWN CHEESE CASSEROLE

2—12 oz. pkg. frozen,
   hashed brown potatoes
2 cups sour cream
1 can cream of chicken
   soup (cream of celery or
   cream of mushroom,
   depending on what you
   have!)
1 stick butter or margarine,
   melted
1 tsp. salt
1 Tbsp. minced onion
2 cups shredded cheddar
   cheese
2 cups corn flakes, crushed
¼ cup butter, melted

SERVES 8
Thaw potatoes and drain well. Combine sour cream, soup and butter. Mix well and add salt, onion, and cheese. Blend in potatoes and stir well. Pour mixture into shallow, 2 quart casserole. Mix corn flakes and ¼ cup melted butter and sprinkle on top of potatoes. Bake, uncovered, at 350° for about 50 minutes or until brown and bubbly.

VEGETABLES, RICE & PASTA

CATTLEMEN'S CLUB TWICE-BAKED POTATOES

5 large potatoes, scrubbed
and baked
⅓ cup half and half
1 cup sour cream
3 Tbsp. green onions or
chives, minced
4 strips bacon, fried and
crumbled
½ tsp. parsley
1 cup cheddar cheese,
grated
1½-2 tsp. salt
½ tsp. pepper
¼ tsp. garlic salt
1 egg, beaten
⅓ cup butter
½ cup mushrooms, sliced
and sauteed in butter

SERVES 8-10
Bake potatoes for one hour at 350° or until tender in center. Cut in half lengthwise. Scoop out potato carefully as to not tear skins. Mash potatoes with mixer, add half and half and continue to beat until smooth. Add all other ingredients and mix well. Mixture should be somewhat softer than regular mashed potatoes to prevent drying out when baking again. Fill skin shells with mashed potato mixture and arrange on cookie sheet. Top each with extra grated cheese. Bake at 350° for 20 minutes. Great with steaks!

CATHY'S PARIS POTATOES

6 medium potatoes
2 cups creamed cottage
cheese
1 cup sour cream
4 green onions and tops,
finely chopped
½ tsp. garlic salt
Salt and pepper to taste
1 cup cheddar cheese,
shredded

SERVES 6
Cook potatoes in boiling salted water until tender, but not soft. Drain, cool, and peel. Cut into ½ inch cubes. Combine potatoes with cottage cheese, sour cream, onions, garlic salt, and salt and pepper. Bake uncovered in a greased 2 quart casserole at 350°for 20 minutes. Sprinkle cheese on top and bake an additional 10 minutes.

VEGETABLES, RICE & PASTA

SPINACH SOUFFLE WITH MUSHROOM SAUCE

1 pkg. fresh spinach or
1—10 oz. pkg. frozen
chopped spinach
2 Tbsp. butter
¼ cup minced green onion
2 eggs
2 egg yolks
1 cup half and half
½ cup bread crumbs
3 Tbsp. Parmesan cheese

SAUCE:
2 Tbsp. butter
½-¾ lb. mushrooms
1 cup whipping cream
Salt and pepper
1 Tbsp. butter
1 Tbsp. flour
2 Tbsp. minced chives

SERVES 4-6
Cook fresh spinach 2-3 minutes. Drain, squeeze out water and mince. If using frozen spinach, cook for 3-5 minutes and drain. Melt 2 tablespoons butter in small skillet. Saute onion. Combine onion and spinach in large bowl. Mix together the eggs, yolks, and half and half. Add to spinach mixture along with bread crumbs and Parmesan cheese. Turn into 8 x 8 inch baking dish and bake in water bath (set baking dish in larger pan with 1 inch of water). Cover with foil. Bake 50 minutes at 350° or until knife comes out clean.

To prepare sauce, melt butter in small saucepan and saute mushrooms. Add cream and bring to boil. Melt 1 tablespoon butter in a cup and add 1 tablespoon flour. Mix to make a paste. Whisk paste into the boiling cream; reduce heat and mix hard until smooth. Salt and pepper to taste. Spoon over souffle and sprinkle with chives or pour sauce into gravy boat and pass separately. This is a rich and elegant vegetable dish.

VEGETABLES, RICE & PASTA

EASY YELLOW SQUASH

Yellow squash or zucchini
Salt
Pepper
Butter
1 jar Kraft's Jalapeno
    Cheeze Whiz
Paprika

This recipe is a "do it by looking" one. The amount of squash you start out with regulates how much cheese you use. Wash and cut squash. Boil in water until done. Drain well. Add butter, salt and pepper to taste. Stir in Jalapeno Cheeze Whiz until it is melted. Put in buttered casserole and sprinkle with paprika. Bake uncovered at 350° until it bubbles. This is a good, easy way to fix squash.

MEXICAN SQUASH CASSEROLE

2 lbs. yellow or zucchini
    squash, or
3—10 oz. pkg. frozen
    squash
½ onion, chopped
¼ cup butter or
    margarine
1 cup grated longhorn
    cheese
3 eggs, beaten
1 small can evaporated milk
3 Tbsp. chopped green
    chilies
2 cups cracker crumbs
1—2 oz. jar pimentos
Salt and pepper to taste
Grated cheese to cover

SERVES 6-8
Wash squash and slice thin. Partially cover with water, add chopped onion and cook 15 minutes. Drain well and add ¼ cup margarine, grated cheese and beaten eggs. While squash is cooking, pour 1 can evaporated milk over cracker crumbs. When soft, add to squash mixture. Add green chilies, pimentos, salt and pepper and bake uncovered 35 minutes at 325°. Remove from oven, cover generously with cheese and bake 10 more minutes.

 Tomatoes peel easily if dipped for a few seconds in scalding water.

VEGETABLES, RICE & PASTA

SAUTEED SQUASH WITH MUSHROOMS AND ONIONS

3 slices bacon
2-3 zucchini and/or yellow
   summer squash
1 small onion, chopped
½ cup fresh mushrooms,
   whole or sliced
1 tomato
1/8 tsp. salt
Parmesan cheese

SERVES 4

Cook bacon in skillet until crisp. Drain and remove all fat from skillet, except enough to cover bottom of pan. Cut washed squash into 1/8 inch rounds. Saute in bacon fat along with onions and mushrooms until tender. Cut tomato into 6-8 lengthwise slices. Add tomato and crumbled bacon to squash mixture and heat well. Add salt. Turn into serving bowl and sprinkle with Parmesan cheese. Serve with extra Parmesan cheese for individual flavoring. This is a good summertime vegetable dish, especially with barbecued chicken, Onion Bread, and Homemade Vanilla Ice Cream.

BROILED TOMATOES

4 medium size tomatoes,
   cut in half
1 cup bread crumbs
2 Tbsp. butter
Parmesan cheese
Parsley
Salt and pepper to taste

SERVES 4

Place each tomato half on a greased pan. Saute bread crumbs in butter until crisp. Pile bread crumbs on top of tomatoes; sprinkle Parmesan cheese on each. Season with salt and pepper. Place in a 350° oven and bake until tomatoes are soft, about 20-25 minutes. Add a sprig of fresh parsley to each tomato before serving. These are good with ham, Macaroni, Mushroom, Green Bean Casserole and Lemon Pudding Cake for dessert.

VEGETABLES, RICE & PASTA

SPINACH-STUFFED TOMATOES

6 small tomatoes, top ¼
   cut off
½ cup cottage cheese
2 Tbsp. plain yogurt
½ tsp. salt
Dash of pepper
Dash of nutmeg
1—10 oz. pkg. frozen
   chopped spinach, cooked
   and drained well
1 Tbsp. minced fresh onion
2 Tbsp. bread crumbs

SERVES 6
Scoop out tomato seeds and some of the pulp from each tomato. Sprinkle tomato shells with salt and turn upside down to drain. Using blender or food processor, blend cottage cheese, yogurt, ½ tsp. salt, pepper and nutmeg. Mix with spinach, onion, and 1 tablespoon bread crumbs. Spoon mixture into tomato shells and sprinkle with remaining bread crumbs. Place on baking sheet and cook 15-20 minutes at 400°.

CHEESE SAUCE FOR VEGETABLES

3 Tbsp. butter
2 Tbsp. flour
¾ cup half and half
½ cup cheddar cheese,
   grated
¼ tsp. salt
Pepper

Melt butter in small saucepan. Add flour and stir well to make paste. Add half and half. Cook over medium heat, stirring constantly until smooth and thick. Add cheese and cook until melted. Pour over cooked broccoli, cauliflower, or asparagus.

VEGETABLES, RICE & PASTA

HOT CURRIED FRUIT

¼ cup melted margarine
½ cup brown sugar
2 Tbsp. cornstarch
1 Tbsp. curry powder
1—1 lb. can sliced pears,
  well drained
1—1 lb. can sliced
  peaches, well drained
1—1 lb. can pineapple
  chunks, well drained
1—8 oz. bottle maraschino
  cherries, well drained
1 cup black pitted cherries
2 bananas, cut in large
  pieces

SERVES 8
Melt butter in a saucepan; add sugar, cornstarch, and curry powder. Stir until smooth. Mix drained fruit in a 2 quart casserole. Pour sauce over fruit and toss lightly. Bake 40 minutes, uncovered, at 350°. This dish is excellent with a baked ham, or with Chicken and Dressing Casserole.

FRIED APPLE RINGS

4 large, tart, cooking
  apples, cored
3 Tbsp. butter
⅓ cup brown sugar
½ tsp. ground cinnamon
  or nutmeg
2 Tbsp. water

SERVES 4-6
Cut apples into ¼ inch thick rounds. Heat butter in large cast iron skillet. Over moderate heat, saute apple rings 3-5 minutes, or until they begin to soften. Sprinkle remaining ingredients, in the order given, and continue to cook 5-7 minutes. Spoon syrup over apples until they are tender and coated with juice. Serve these at brunch or as an accompaniment to ham. These are a real Southern treat!

VEGETABLES, RICE & PASTA

FRIED RICE WITH BACON AND MUSHROOMS

3 Tbsp. bacon drippings
½ cup green onions and
  tops
1 cup celery, diced
1 cup mushrooms, sliced
3 cups cooked rice
  (cooled)
2 Tbsp. soy sauce
1 egg, slightly beaten
½ lb. bacon, fried and
  crumbled

SERVES 6
Saute onions and celery in bacon drippings. Cook until tender. Add mushrooms, rice and soy sauce. Cook 10 minutes on low heat, stirring occasionally. Stir in beaten egg and cook only until egg is done. Add bacon and mix well. Serve this with extra soy sauce. This is a good accompaniment for Sweet and Sour Pork.

EASY RICE

2—10½ oz. cans beef
  consomme
¾ stick butter or margarine
1 small onion, chopped
1—4 oz. can sliced
  mushrooms, drained
1 cup raw rice (not quick)

SERVES 6
Combine ingredients in a casserole and bake uncovered at 325° for 1 hour. You can increase the heat if you want to speed up cooking time or cover if it is cooking too fast.

RICE AND CHILIES

¾ cup Uncle Ben's Rice
  (or any quick cooking
  rice)
Salt to taste
1—6 oz. can chopped
  green chilies
2 cups sour cream
½ lb. Monterey Jack
  cheese, grated
Butter

SERVES 4-5
Cook rice. Combine with sour cream and salt. Arrange half of this mixture in lightly-greased casserole. Place green chilies and half of grated cheese on top. Add the rest of rice mixture. Cover with dots of butter and remaining cheese. Bake uncovered at 350° for 30 minutes.

VEGETABLES, RICE & PASTA

MACARONI, MUSHROOMS AND GREEN BEANS

1 pkg. Kraft Macaroni
and Cheese Deluxe
1—4 oz. can sliced
mushrooms, drained
1—1 lb. can green beans,
drained

SERVES 8
Prepare macaroni and cheese according to package directions. While
still in saucepan, add mushrooms and
green beans (you can add more to
suit your taste or use cooked fresh or
frozen green beans). Pour mixture
into a 2 quart casserole and sprinkle
with paprika. Bake uncovered for
10-15 minutes in a 350° oven. This
is so easy and delicious . . . it makes
an excellent accompaniment for ham
or pork chops. Kids love it.

MACARONI AND CHEESE DELUXE

2 cups elbow macaroni
2 quarts boiling water
1 Tbsp. salt
2 Tbsp. butter
2 Tbsp. chopped onion
2 Tbsp. flour
Salt and pepper
2 cups milk
3 cups sharp American
cheese, grated
Parsley
1½ tsp. Worcestershire

SERVES 6
Add 1 tablespoon salt to boiling
water; add macaroni and cook until
tender. Drain. Saute onion in 2 tablespoons melted butter until tender. Stir
in flour, salt and pepper. Add milk and
stir over low heat until slightly thick
and smooth. Add 2 cups of grated
cheese, parsley and Worcestershire
sauce. Cook slowly until cheese
melts. Combine with macaroni. Pour
into 2 quart buttered casserole. Top
with remaining cup of grated cheese.
Bake uncovered until bubbly, about
30 minutes. This old family recipe is a
real winner.

*Always cook cheese at low temperature. Cheese become
tough or stringy if cooked too fast or too long.*

Desserts

DESSERTS

FRESH APPLE CAKE

1 cup oil
2 cups sugar
2 eggs
2¼ cups flour
1 tsp. baking soda
1 tsp. salt
1 tsp. cinnamon
½ tsp. nutmeg
3 cups apples, peeled and
   chopped
1 cup nuts, chopped
1 tsp. vanilla

ICING:
1 stick butter or margarine
1 cup brown sugar
¼ cup evaporated milk

Combine oil and sugar. Add eggs and beat well. Sift dry ingredients into mixture and mix well. Stir in apples, nuts, and vanilla. Blend well. Bake in greased and floured tube pan at 350° for 1½ hours. Makes a large cake that freezes well.

Blend icing ingredients in saucepan. Boil for 2 minutes. Pour over cake while hot. Let icing soak into cake while pouring. Remove from pan when cool.

BLACK BOTTOM CUPCAKES

8 oz. cream cheese
½ cup sugar
1 egg
1/8 tsp. salt
6 oz. semi-sweet
   chocolate bits
1½ cups flour
1 cup sugar
¼ cup cocoa
1 tsp. soda
½ tsp. salt
⅓ cup oil
1 Tbsp. vinegar
1 cup water
1 tsp. vanilla

MAKES 18-20
Soften cream cheese and add sugar, egg and salt. Mix well with beater. Stir in chocolate bits. In separate bowl, combine all other ingredients. Mix well. Fill greased or lined muffin tins ½ full with chocolate mixture. Drop large teaspoonfuls of cream cheese mixture in center of each cupcake. Bake at 350° for 25-30 minutes or until white center is slightly brown. These don't need frosting.

BLARNEY STONES

4 eggs, separated
1 cup sugar
1 cup flour + 2 Tbsp.
1¼ tsp. baking powder
¼ tsp. salt
½ cup boiling water
½ tsp. vanilla

FROSTING:
1 egg yolk (reserved from
   the cake recipe)
1 cup butter, softened
2½ cups powdered sugar
1 tsp. vanilla
Crushed salted peanuts

Separate eggs, reserving 1 yolk for icing. Beat remaining yolks until thick and lemon colored. Add sugar gradually, beating continuously. Add dry ingredients, sifted together, alternating with boiling water. Add vanilla and beat well. Fold in stiffly beaten egg whites. Bake 30 minutes at 350° in 13 x 9 inch pan. When cool, ice with Blarney Stone Frosting, and cut into squares.

To make frosting, cream together egg yolk, butter and sugar until soft and smooth. Add vanilla. Ice cake and sprinkle crushed salted peanuts on top. Make as a special treat for St. Patrick's Day!!

BROWNIE PUDDING CAKE

1 cup flour
¾ cup sugar
2 Tbsp. cocoa
2 tsp. baking powder
½ tsp. salt
½ cup milk
1 tsp. vanilla
2 Tbsp. oil
¾ cup walnuts
¾ cup brown sugar
¼ cup cocoa
1¾ cup hot water

Mix flour, sugar, cocoa, baking powder, salt, milk, vanilla and oil in bowl. Pour into greased 8 x 8 inch pan. Combine walnuts, brown sugar and cocoa in bowl. Add boiling water to nut mixture and mix well. Pour over batter mixture in pan. Bake at 350° for 45 minutes. Good with vanilla ice cream on top.

DESSERTS

CARROT CAKE

2 cups flour
2 cups sugar
2 tsp. cinnamon
1 tsp. salt
2 tsp. soda
1 cup oil
4 eggs
3 cups grated carrots
1 tsp. vanilla

FROSTING:
1—8 oz. pkg. cream cheese
1 lb. powdered sugar
1 stick butter or margarine
1-2 Tbsp. milk
1 tsp. vanilla
1 cup chopped nuts

Mix dry ingredients. Add oil and vanilla and mix well. Add eggs, one at a time, beating after each egg. Stir in grated carrots. Bake at 350° for 45-60 minutes in a greased and floured 9 x 13 inch pan or in two 9-inch round cake pans.

To make the frosting, cream together cream cheese and butter, blend in powdered sugar and vanilla. Add enough milk to make smooth. Stir in nuts.

CHOCOLATE SHEET CAKE

2 cups flour
2 cups sugar
1 stick margarine
1 cup cold water
4 Tbsp. cocoa
½ cup salad oil
½ cup buttermilk
2 eggs, beaten
1 tsp. soda
1 tsp. vanilla

FROSTING:
1 stick margarine
4 Tbsp. cocoa
6-7 Tbsp. milk
1 lb. powdered sugar
1 tsp. vanilla
1 cup pecans, chopped

In large bowl, combine flour and sugar. In saucepan, combine margarine, water, cocoa, and salad oil. Bring to a boil. Remove from heat, and pour immediately over the flour/sugar mixture. Mix well. Add buttermilk, eggs, soda, and vanilla. Mix well. Pour into well-greased jelly roll pan (17x11x1) and bake 20 minutes at 400°. (You can use a 9 x 13 inch pan, but increase the cooking time.) While cake is in the oven, combine margarine, cocoa, and milk in a saucepan. Bring to a boil. Remove from heat and add powdered sugar, vanilla and nuts. Mix well. Pour over hot cake. From start to finish, this cake takes about 25-30 minutes to make. It is easy, delicious and makes enough to feed a large group of people. It also freezes nicely. After trying this cake, you will never mess with another chocolate layer cake!

QUICK CHOCOLATE-CHERRY CAKE

1 chocolate cake mix
1 can cherry pie filling
2 eggs

FROSTING:
⅓ cup milk
1 cup sugar
5 Tbsp. butter
1 cup chocolate chips

Combine chocolate cake mix, pie filling and two eggs in bowl. Mix well. Pour into greased and floured 9 x 13 inch pan and bake at 350° for 25 minutes or until done to touch.

In saucepan, combine milk, sugar and butter. Heat to boiling and boil 1 minute, stirring constantly. Add chocolate chips and stir well. Let sit for 10-15 minutes, stirring occasionally. Pour warm frosting over cake—will be somewhat runny. This cakes keeps better in the refrigerator. It's an easy and quick cake for spur-of-the-moment guests.

CHOCOLATE CHIP CAKE

1½ cups boiling water
1 cup oatmeal
1 cup brown sugar
1 cup white sugar
½ cup shortening
2 eggs
1½ cup flour
1 tsp. soda
½ tsp. salt
1 Tbsp. cocoa
1 cup chocolate chips
½ cup nuts, chopped

Pour boiling water over oatmeal in small bowl. Stir and let stand 10 minutes. Cream sugars and shortening in separate bowl; add eggs and beat until smooth. Add oatmeal and mix well. Add flour, soda, salt and cocoa. Beat 1 minute. Stir in ½ cup chocolate chips. Pour into greased and floured 8 x 12 inch pan. Sprinke ½ cup chocolate chips and ½ cup nuts over top. Bake at 350° for 35-40 minutes.

 Powdered buttermilk is great to have on hand for those recipes that call for buttermilk, especially if you're not a buttermilk drinker.

DESSERTS

CREAMY LAYERED CHOCOLATE MINT CAKE

1 chocolate mint cake mix
1½ large containers
    whipped topping
1/8 cup creme de menthe
    (optional)
2 tsp. mint flavoring
Green food coloring

CHOCOLATE SAUCE:
½ cup sugar
4 tsp. cornstarch
½ cup water
1—1 oz. square
    unsweetened
    chocolate
Dash salt
1 Tbsp. butter
½ tsp. vanilla

Make cake according to directions on box. Pour into 2 layer pans. After baking, remove from pans and freeze. Cut each layer in half while partially frozen, making 4 layers. Add 1/8 cup creme de menthe and the flavoring to whipped topping. Tint with green food coloring. Frost each layer generously with whip cream mixture. Refrigerate. Cake moistens and is better if it can sit at least several hours before serving. Drizzle chocolate sauce over each serving.

To prepare sauce, combine ½ cup sugar and the cornstarch in saucepan. Add water, chocolate and salt. Cook and stir until thickened and bubbly. Remove from heat; stir in butter and vanilla.

CHOCOLATE POUND CAKE

1 cup margarine
½ cup Crisco
3 cups sugar
5 eggs
2 tsp. vanilla
½ cup cocoa
3 cups flour
½ tsp. salt
1 tsp. baking powder
1 cup milk
Powdered sugar, optional

Heat oven to 325°. Grease and flour Bundt pan. Sift flour, salt and baking powder together. Set aside. Cream margarine, Crisco and sugar until fluffy. Add eggs, vanilla and cocoa; beat until smooth. Add sifted dry ingredients alternately with milk, beginning and ending with dry ingredients. Mix well. Take out 2 cups batter and make cupcakes (bake only 30-45 minutes), and pour rest of batter in a greased and floured Bundt pan. Bake at least 1 hour or until done. Cool before removing from pan. Sift powdered sugar onto cake, just before serving. This cake freezes well, and is better 1 or 2 days after it is made as it becomes more moist.

SPICED CHOCOLATE ZUCCHINI CAKE

2½ cups unsifted flour
½ cup unsweetened cocoa
1¾ tsp. baking powder
1½ tsp. soda
1 tsp. salt
¾ cup butter or margarine, softened
2 cups minus 2 Tbsp. sugar
2 tsp. cinnamon
¾ tsp. nutmeg
3 extra large eggs
2 cups shredded, unpeeled zucchini
2 tsp. vanilla
½ cup plus 2 Tbsp. milk

FROSTING:
1—3 oz. pkg. cream cheese, softened
⅓ cup butter or margarine, softened
¾ tsp. cinnamon
4 cups powdered sugar
1 tsp. vanilla
1½-2 Tbsp. milk

Mix flour, cocoa, baking powder, soda and salt. In large bowl, cream butter, sugar, cinnamon and nutmeg until light. Add eggs, mixing well. Stir in zucchini and vanilla. Mix well. Add dry ingredients alternately with milk beginning and ending with flour. Beat well after each addition. Pour batter into two 9-inch layer cake pans, which have been greased and floured (or a 9 x 13 inch oblong pan). Bake at 375° about 30 minutes for round cake pans or 40 minutes for oblong, or until toothpick inserted in middle comes out clean. Cool, then ice with cream cheese frosting.

To make frosting, beat together cream cheese, butter and cinnamon until smooth. Gradually add powdered sugar, mixing until smooth. Stir in vanilla. Gradually add milk until it is the right consistency for spreading. Ice the cake and enjoy! This is a very moist cake that keeps well.

Use cocoa instead of flour when preparing pan for chocolate cake.

GERMAN CHOCOLATE CAKE

1—4 oz. pkg. German's
   sweet chocolate
½ cup boiling water
1 cup butter
2 cups sugar
4 egg yolks
1 tsp. vanilla
2¼ cups sifted flour
1 tsp. baking soda
½ tsp. salt
1 cup buttermilk
4 egg whites, stiffly
   beaten

**COCONUT PECAN
FROSTING:**
¾ cup evaporated milk
½ cup brown sugar
½ cup sugar
½ cup butter
1 tsp. vanilla
3 egg yolks
1½ cups coconut
1 cup pecans, chopped

Melt the chocolate in the boiling water and let cool. Cream butter and sugar, add yolks, beating well after each. Blend in vanilla and chocolate. Sift flour with salt and soda. Add to chocolate mixture alternating with buttermilk. Beat until smooth. Fold in beaten egg whites. Pour into three 9-inch layer pans, lined with wax paper. Bake at 350° for 30-35 minutes. Cool and frost with Coconut-Pecan Frosting.

Frosting: Combine milk, sugars, butter, and vanilla in saucepan. Bring to full boil, stirring constantly. Remove from heat. Mixture may appear curdled. Quickly stir small amount of hot mixture into beaten egg yolks. Stir this back into saucepan with rest of hot mixture. Return to a boil, stirring constantly. Remove from heat. Add coconut and pecans. Cool, beating occasionally. Ice cake layers when cool.

DEE'S YELLOW COCONUT CAKE

1 pkg. yellow cake mix
1 small pkg. vanilla instant
  pudding
1¾ cup water
4 eggs
¼ cup oil
2 cups coconut
1 cup walnuts or pecans,
  chopped

FROSTING:
4 Tbsp. butter
2 cups coconut
1—8 oz. pkg. cream
  cheese
2 tsp. milk
3½ cups powdered sugar
½ tsp. vanilla

Combine first five ingredients and beat for 4 minutes. Stir in coconut and nuts. Pour into 3 greased and floured 9-inch pans. Bake for 35 minutes at 350°. Cool in pans and remove.

To make frosting, melt 2 tablespoons butter in skillet. Add 2 cups coconut. Stir over low heat until brown and toasted. In bowl, cream softened cheese and 2 tablespoons butter. Add milk, powdered sugar and vanilla. Mix until smooth. Stir in 1¾ cup of the toasted coconut. Frost cake. Sprinkle remaining ¼ cup toasted coconut on sides and top.

MOIST COCONUT CAKE

1 pkg. yellow cake mix
1½ cups milk
½ cup sugar
1½ cups coconut
3½ cups prepared whipped
  topping, thawed

Prepare cake mix as directed on package, baking in 9 x 13 inch pan. Cool cake 15 minutes. Poke holes down through cake with utility fork. In saucepan combine milk, sugar and ½ cup coconut. Bring to boil, reduce heat and simmer 1 minute. Mixture will be runny. Carefully spoon over warm cake, allowing liquid to soak down through holes. Cool completely. Fold ½ cup of the coconut into whipped topping and spread over cake. Toast remaining ½ cup coconut and sprinkle on top of whipped topping. Chill. Store cake in refrigerator.

COOKIE CAKE

2 cups flour
2 cups sugar
1 tsp. soda
3½ Tbsp. chocolate syrup
1 stick margarine
1 cup water
⅓ cup buttermilk
2 eggs
1 tsp. vanilla

FROSTING:
1 stick margarine
3½ Tbsp. chocolate syrup
⅓ cup milk
1 lb. powdered sugar
1 tsp. vanilla
1 cup nuts, chopped

Mix flour, sugar, and soda in large bowl. Combine chocolate syrup, margarine and water in saucepan and bring to a boil. Cool boiled mixture slightly and pour over the flour mixture. Add buttermilk, eggs and vanilla, beating well. Pour into a 11 x 16 inch jelly roll pan that has been greased and floured. Bake 20 minutes at 400°.

To make frosting, boil margarine, chocolate syrup and milk. Remove from heat, add powdered sugar. Stir in vanilla and nuts. Put on cake as soon as it comes out of the oven. This cake won't last long, as it is really delicious!

EILEEN'S ITALIAN CREAM CAKE

½ cup Crisco
½ cup butter or margarine
1⅔ cup sugar
5 eggs, separated
1 cup buttermilk
¾ tsp. baking soda
½ tsp. salt
2 cups flour, sifted
1 tsp. vanilla
1 cup pecans, chopped
1—3½ oz. can coconut

CREAM CHEESE
FROSTING:
8 oz. cream cheese, softened
¼ cup margarine, softened
1 lb. powdered sugar
1 tsp. vanilla
1-2 Tbsp. milk
1 cup chopped pecans

Cream margarine and Crisco; add sugar gradually and beat until fluffy. Add egg yolks, one at a time and beat well after each addition. Add buttermilk alternately with dry ingredients starting and ending with flour. Stir in vanilla, pecans, and coconut. Fold in stiffly-beaten egg whites. Bake in 3 greased and floured 9 inch layer pans at 350° for 30-40 minutes or until done. Cool before removing from pan. Ice with Cream Cheese Frosting.

To make frosting, cream cheese and margarine until smooth. Add remaining ingredients, ending with milk to make the proper spreading consistency. Stir in nuts if desired.

LEMON PUDDING CAKE

3 Tbsp. butter
1 cup sugar
4 eggs, separated
3 Tbsp. flour
¼ tsp. salt
⅓ cup lemon juice
1 cup milk
2 tsp. grated lemon peel
¼ cup sliced almonds
Nutmeg

Cream butter and sugar in bowl. Add egg yolks and beat. Add flour, salt, lemon juice, milk and lemon peel. Mix well. In separate bowl, beat egg whites until stiff. Fold into batter. Pour into 6 x 8 inch buttered dish. Sprinkle almonds over batter. Set in water bath for baking. Bake at 325° for 50-55 minutes. Dust with nutmeg. This will be a favorite!

MISSISSIPPI MUD CAKE

2 sticks margarine
2 cups sugar
4 eggs
1 tsp. vanilla
2 Tbsp. cocoa
1½ cups flour
1 cup nuts, chopped
1 cup coconut

FROSTING:
1 small jar marshmallow
   creme
1—1 lb. box powdered
   sugar
1 stick margarine, softened
½ cup evaporated milk
⅓ cup cocoa
1 tsp. vanilla

Cream margarine and sugar. Add eggs and vanilla and beat well. Combine cocoa, flour, nuts and coconut in bowl and mix with spoon. Add to other ingredients. Mix well. Pour into greased 9 x 13 inch pan. Bake at 350° for 35-45 minutes.

Frosting: Spoon marshmallow creme over warm cake. Let soften, then spread over cake. Blend softened margarine with sugar; add other ingredients, mixing well. Spread over marshmallow layer. This cake is too good to be true!

 Cake layers will come out of their pans without sticking if you set the hot pans on a damp cloth when they come out of the oven.

DESSERTS

MOCHA BALLS

4 eggs, separated
1 cup sugar
1 cup flour plus 2 Tbsp.
1¼ tsp. baking powder
¼ tsp. salt
½ cup boiling water
¼ tsp. vanilla

FROSTING:
1 lb. powdered sugar
1 stick butter, softened
5 Tbsp. cocoa
2 tsp. vanilla
4-5 Tbsp. evaporated milk
1 lb. pecans, finely ground

MAKES 36 SQUARES

Separate eggs. Beat yolks until thick and lemon colored. Add sugar gradually, beating continuously. Add dry ingredients, sifted together, alternately with boiling water. Add vanilla and beat well. Fold in stiffly beaten egg whites. Bake 30 minutes at 350° in a 13 x 9 inch pan. When cool, cut into 36 squares.

Make a frosting of sugar, butter, cocoa, vanilla, and canned milk. Heat in double boiler until runny for spreading. Spread all six sides of the sponge cake squares (messy, but worth it) and roll all sides in finely chopped nuts. This is a very old recipe from Germany. It isn't an easy one and it takes time, but it is great for festive occasions. You might think of making mocha balls a part of your Christmas tradition!

ORANGE KISS ME CAKE

1 large orange
½ cup milk
1 cup raisins
⅓ cup walnuts, chopped
2 cups flour
1 cup sugar
1 tsp. soda
1 tsp. salt
½ cup oil
¾ cup milk
2 eggs
⅓ cup orange juice
⅓ cup sugar
1 tsp. cinnamon
¼ cup walnuts, chopped

Squeeze juice from orange. Combine pulp and rind in blender with ½ cup milk to puree. Mix with raisins and walnuts. Sift together flour, sugar, soda, and salt. Add oil and ¾ cup milk. Beat 1½ minutes. Add eggs and beat another minute. Fold in orange-raisin mixture. Pour into 12x8x2 inch greased and floured pan. Bake at 350° for 40-50 minutes. Meanwhile combine ⅓ cup orange juice, ⅓ cup sugar, 1 teaspoon cinnamon, and ¼ cup walnuts. Pour mixture over warm cake.

PINEAPPLE UPSIDE-DOWN CAKE

½ cup butter
1 cup packed brown sugar
1—20 oz. can sliced
   pineapple, drained
Maraschino cherries
1 Supermoist Betty
   Crocker Yellow cake mix,
   or White Cake (below)
12 pecan halves

WHITE CAKE:
3 cups flour
2 cups sugar
3 tsp. baking powder
1 tsp. salt
1½ cups milk
⅔ cup shortening
2 eggs
2 tsp. vanilla

Melt butter in 9 x 13 inch pan. Sprinkle brown sugar over butter. Arrange pineapple slices in butter/brown sugar mixture. Place a maraschino cherry in center of each pineapple slice. Scatter pecan halves between pineapple slices. Prepare cake mix as directed on the package. If making White Cake, combine all ingredients in bowl and mix well. Pour batter over pineapple. Bake 45-55 minutes at 350°. As soon as it is taken out of the oven, invert onto a serving plate. Serve with whipped cream. This recipe can be easily halved and baked in a round layer pan for 35-40 minutes.

MOTHER LINK'S 7-UP POUND CAKE

2 sticks margarine
½ cup Crisco
3 cups sugar
5 eggs
3 cups flour
2 Tbsp. vanilla
1 tsp. lemon extract
1—7 oz. bottle 7-Up

LEMON GLAZE:
1 cup powdered sugar
Juice of 1 lemon

Do not use cake flour or sift. Stir flour in cannister before measuring. Cream margarine and Crisco. Add sugar slowly and eggs one at a time, beating well after each addition. Add other ingredients except 7-Up and mix well. Slowly add 7-Up, mixing well. Pour into greased and floured Bundt pan and bake 1 hour and 20 minutes at 350°. Let cake sit until cool, then invert onto a cake plate. Drizzle glaze over cake. Freezes well.

Raisins heated a moment in the oven will not sink to the bottom of the cake.

STRAWBERRY CAKE

1 Duncan Hines white
   cake mix
1—3 oz. pkg. strawberry
   jello
¾ box (10 oz.) frozen
   strawberries, thawed
Scant ½ cup oil
½ cup water
4 eggs

STRAWBERRY ICING:
1 lb. powdered sugar
¼ box frozen strawberries,
   thawed
½ stick butter, softened

Mix cake mix, jello, strawberries, oil and water. Beat well. Add eggs, one at a time, beating well after each egg. Pour into 3 greased and floured 9 inch round cake pans (or a 9 x 13 inch cake pan) and bake at 350° for 30-35 minutes for round pans; 35-40 minutes for 9 x 13 inch. Cake is done when toothpick inserted in the middle comes out clean. When cool, frost with Strawberry Icing.

To make the icing, blend softened butter and powdered sugar. Add frozen strawberries and blend well.

APRICOT SOURS

1½ cups flour
⅔ cup butter
¾ cup dried apricots
   (4 oz.)
2 eggs
1 cup brown sugar, packed
½ tsp. vanilla
½ cup pecans

GLAZE:
¾ cup powdered sugar
2 Tbsp. lemon juice

MAKES 3 DOZEN
Cut butter into flour until mixture is coarse. Press into bottom of a 13x9x2 inch pan. Bake at 350° for 10 minutes. Set aside and cool while preparing apricots. Cover apricots with boiling water and simmer 5-10 minutes. Drain and cool. Chop coarsely (use food processor if you have one) and fold into the following egg mixture. Beat eggs until thick; add brown sugar gradually, beating well after each addition. Blend in vanilla. Add pecans and apricots. Pour over dough crust. Bake at 350° for 20-30 minutes or until wooden pick comes out clean. Glaze immediately with mixture of powdered sugar and lemon juice. Cut into squares.

BUTTER SUGAR COOKIES

1 cup butter
1 cup sugar
½ tsp. vanilla
1 egg
2 cups flour
½ tsp. soda
½ tsp. cream of tartar

MAKES 2 DOZEN

Cream butter and sugar. Add vanilla and egg, then sifted dry ingredients Mix thoroughly. Chill dough. Place on cookie sheet in small balls and flatten with fork dipped in sugar, making sure each cookie is sprinkled with sugar. Bake at 350° until edges just begin to turn golden, about 10 minutes.

This is a good recipe for holiday sugar cookies. After the dough is chilled, roll out a portion to ¼ inch thickness. Using your favorite cookie cutters, cut into shapes; sprinkle with colored sugar, and bake. Can also be baked plain and frosted.

FAVORITE CHOCOLATE CHIP COOKIES

½ cup butter or margarine
½ cup Crisco (try the butter-flavored)
¾ cup white sugar
¾ cup brown sugar, packed
1 tsp. vanilla
2 eggs
2¼ cups unsifted flour
1 tsp. baking soda
1 tsp. salt
2 cups chocolate chips (12 oz.)
1 cup chopped nuts (optional)

MAKES 2-3 DOZEN

Cream butter, shortening, sugar, and vanilla. Add eggs and mix well. Add the dry ingredients and stir until thoroughly mixed. Stir in chocolate chips and nuts. Drop by the heaping teaspoonful onto ungreased cookie sheet and bake at 375° for 8-10 minutes or until golden brown. Remove from cookie sheet and cool.

 When rolling cookie dough, use powdered sugar instead of flour on your board. This will make your cookies a wee bit sweeter but they will not get tough as they sometimes do when they are rolled out on a floured board.

181

DESERTS

CHOCOLATE SNOWBALLS

¾ cup butter
½ cup sugar
2 tsp. vanilla
1 egg
2 cups flour
½ tsp. salt
1 cup nuts, chopped
6-oz. chocolate chips
Powdered sugar

MAKES 2 DOZEN
Cream butter and sugar. Add vanilla and egg; mix well. Add flour and salt. Mix well. Stir in chocolate chips and nuts. Roll dough into 1 inch diameter balls and place on greased cookie sheet. Bake for 15-20 minutes in 350° oven. Cool. Roll in powdered sugar.

AUNT VERNA'S DATE COOKIES

2 cups brown sugar
1 cup shortening
2 eggs
3½ cups flour
2 tsp. cream of tartar
1 tsp. soda
1 tsp. salt
1 tsp. vanilla
½ tsp. lemon extract
1 cup chopped dates
1 cup chopped nuts

MAKES 3 DOZEN
Cream sugar and shortening. Add eggs and mix until creamy. Add flour, cream of tartar, soda, salt, vanilla and lemon extract. Mix well. Mix in dates and nuts. Form the dough into a roll, wrap in wax paper, and chill. At this point it can be frozen. Slice off cookies in slices not quite ½ inch thick and bake at 350° for 10-15 minutes.

 When cutting marshmallows or chopping dates, if you dip your scissors into water and cut them wet, the goodies won't stick.

♥■♥■♥■♥■♥■♥■♥■♥■♥■♥■♥■♥■♥■♥■♥■♥■♥

WRANGLER COOKIES

2 large eggs
1 cup sugar
1 cup brown sugar, lightly
  packed
2 sticks butter or margarine
1 tsp. vanilla
1 tsp. soda
½ tsp. baking powder
½ tsp. salt
2 cups flour
2 cups oats
1—6 oz. pkg. chocolate
  chips
¾ cup pecans, chopped
  (optional)

MAKES 2 DOZEN BIG COOKIES

Cream eggs, sugars and butter in a large bowl, until fluffy. Mix in vanilla. Combine dry ingredients and add to creamed mixture. Mix well. Stir in chocolate chips and nuts. The dough will be very stiff. To make an oversize cookie, drop the dough by ¼ cupfuls onto a greased cookie sheet. Put only 6-8 mounds of dough on each sheet as the cookies will spread as they bake. Bake at 350° for 10-15 minutes or until they are golden brown but still spongy on top. Be careful not to overcook, as they are supposed to be chewy. Let cookies cool before removing from the baking sheet. If you prefer a smaller cookie, reduce the baking time accordingly.

HOLLY'S FRUITCAKE COOKIES

2 lb. container of mixed
  candied fruit
1 lb. raisins
1 cup flour
1 cup brown sugar
½ cup margarine
4 eggs
3 Tbsp. buttermilk
½ cup orange juice
1 Tbsp. vanilla
2 cups flour
1 tsp. soda
½ tsp. nutmeg
½ tsp. salt
1½ lb. pecans, whole or
  broken up

MAKES 5 DOZEN

Dust fruit and raisins with 1 cup flour. Cream brown sugar and margarine. Beat in 4 eggs. Add buttermilk, orange juice and vanilla. Mix well. Add 2 cups flour, soda, nutmeg, and salt. Mix well. Add fruit, raisins and nuts. Drop spoonfuls onto greased cookie sheet. Bake at 350° for 14 minutes. Great baked Christmas gift!

DESERTS

KEEPSAKE COOKIES

COOKIES:
2 cups flour
1 cup butter, softened
½ cup sugar
2 tsp. vanilla

PEANUT BUTTER TOPPING:
¼ cup butter
⅓ cup brown sugar
⅓ cup peanut butter

CHOCOLATE GLAZE:
½ cup semi-sweet
   chocolate pieces
2 Tbsp. milk
⅓ cup sifted powdered
   sugar

MAKES 2 DOZEN
Combine flour, butter, sugar and vanilla in bowl. Mix well. Drop by teaspoon onto greased cookie sheet. Flatten with a glass that has been greased on the bottom then dipped in sugar. Bake at 325° for 15-18 minutes. Spread warm cookie with peanut butter topping. Drizzle with chocolate glaze.

To make topping, cream butter, brown sugar and peanut butter. Mix until light and fluffy. To make glaze, melt chocolate pieces with milk in small saucepan over low heat, stirring constantly. Remove from heat. Add powdered sugar; stir until smooth.

PEANUT BUTTER COOKIES

¼ cup butter
¼ cup Crisco
½ cup peanut butter
½ cup sugar
½ cup brown sugar
1 egg, beaten
1 ¼ cups flour
½ tsp. baking powder
¾ tsp. soda
¼ tsp. salt
1 cup chocolate chips
   (optional)

MAKES 3 DOZEN
Cream butter, shortening, peanut butter and sugars until fluffy. Add beaten egg and mix well. Blend in dry ingredients. Chill dough. Roll into 1 inch balls and arrange on cookie sheet. Dip a fork in flour or sugar and flatten each with a crisscross pattern. Bake 10-12 minutes at 350°. (Adding the chocolate chips makes this traditional cookie a bit more interesting.)

POTATO CHIP SHORTBREAD COOKIES

½ lb. butter or margarine
½ cup butter-flavored
   Crisco
1 cup sugar
¾ tsp. vanilla
3 cups flour + 2 Tbsp.
1½ cup crushed potato
   chips
½ cup pecans, chopped
   (optional)
Powdered sugar

MAKES 6-7 DOZEN
Cream butter, shortening and sugar well. Add vanilla and flour, stir in potato chips and nuts, if desired. Drop by teaspoonful onto a greased cookie sheet, and bake at 350° for about 15 minutes or until browned around the edges. These cookies do not spread while cooking, and are very rich; therefore, you can make them small and put them closer together on the pan. When done, dust them lightly with powdered sugar. This is a quick, easy cookie, and anyone who eats them will be amazed they have potato chips in them.

ROLLED OAT COOKIES

1 cup margarine
1 cup brown sugar
1 cup white sugar
2 eggs, beaten
1⅓ cup flour
1 tsp. salt
1 tsp. soda
1 tsp. vanilla
3 cups rolled oats
1 cup Rice Krispies
½ cup chopped nuts

MAKES 6 DOZEN
Cream together margarine and sugars. Add beaten eggs and mix well. Sift dry ingredients together and add to butter/sugar mixture. Add vanilla and mix well. Stir in oats, Rice Krispies and nuts. Chill 2-3 hours and roll into 1 inch balls and set on a cookie sheet 2 inches apart. Bake at 350° for about 10 minutes or until golden brown.

Keep cake and cookies moist by placing a piece of bread or apple in the container.

DESSERTS

SNICKERDOODLES

1 cup shortening
1½ cups sugar
2 eggs
2¾ cup flour, sifted
2 tsp. cream of tartar
1 tsp. soda
½ tsp. salt
2 Tbsp. sugar
2 tsp. cinnamon

MAKES 2-3 DOZEN
Cream together shortening, sugar, and eggs. Sift together and stir in flour, cream of tartar, soda and salt. Shape dough into balls the size of walnuts. Roll each in mixture of the sugar and cinnamon. Place 2 inches apart on ungreased cookie sheet. Bake 8-10 minutes at 400°, or until lightly browned.

BEST-EVER THUMB PRINT COOKIES

1 cup butter
½ cup brown sugar
2 egg yolks
1 tsp. vanilla
2 cups flour
½ tsp. salt
2 egg whites, slightly
   beaten
Finely chopped nuts
Butter cream frosting
Crabapple jelly or
   maraschino cherries

MAKES 30-36 COOKIES
Cream butter and brown sugar. Add yolks and vanilla, mix well. Stir in flour and salt. Roll into 1 inch balls. Dip each ball into egg whites then roll in chopped nuts. Bake 5 minutes at 375°. Make thumbprint in center of each cookie. Bake 8 minutes longer. At Christmas, these are pretty filled with green Butter Cream Frosting and topped with a spoonful of crabapple jelly or a maraschino cherry.

BUTTER CREAM FROSTING:
⅓ cup soft butter
3 cups powdered sugar
1½ tsp. vanilla
2-3 Tbsp. milk

Frosting: Cream butter and sugar, stir in vanilla and add enough milk to make frosting smooth and spreading consistency.

EVERYBODY'S FAVORITE BROWNIES

4 eggs beaten
1 cup sugar
½ cup oil
½ tsp. salt
1 lb. can Hershey's syrup
1 cup plus 2 Tbsp. flour
1 tsp. vanilla
½ cup nuts, chopped

FROSTING:
¼ cup milk
¼ cup oleo
1 cup sugar
1 tsp. vanilla
½ cup chocolate chips

MAKES 2 DOZEN
Combine all ingredients in bowl. Mix well. Pour into 9 x 11 inch greased pan and bake at 350° for 20-25 minutes. Frost when cool.

To make frosting, combine milk, oleo and sugar in small saucepan. Heat to boiling and boil 1 minute. Remove from heat; add vanilla and chocolate chips. Let cool, stirring occasionally.

CHOCO-MINT BARS

FIRST LAYER:
2 oz. unsweetened
   chocolate
½ cup butter
2 eggs
1 cup sugar
½ cup sifted flour

SECOND LAYER:
1½ cups powdered sugar
3 Tbsp. butter
2-3 Tbsp. cream
1 tsp. peppermint extract

THIRD LAYER:
3 oz. semi-sweet or
   unsweetened chocolate
3 Tbsp. butter

MAKES 16 BARS
To make first layer, melt chocolate and butter. Cream eggs with sugar. Add flour and chocolate mixture, mixing well. Pour into 8 x 8 inch pan, bake at 350° for 20 minutes. Turn off oven and let sit an additional 5 minutes.

To prepare second layer, cream sugar and butter. Add other ingredients and mix well. Spread on cooled first layer. Chill. (This layer is prettier tinted green or red.)

For third layer, melt chocolate and butter and pour over peppermint layer.

Add grated orange peel instead of nuts to fudge or brownies for a new treat.

DESSERTS

PEGGY'S LEMON BARS

CRUST:
2 cups flour
1 cup butter, melted
½ cup powdered sugar

FILLING:
4 eggs
2 cups granulated sugar
1 tsp. baking powder
4 Tbsp. flour
6 Tbsp. lemon juice

MAKES 2-3 DOZEN
Mix crust ingredients. Press into greased 9 x 13 inch glass baking dish, leaving edges some higher than center. Bake at 350° for 20-25 minutes or until crust begins to brown.

To make filling, combine all ingredients and mix well with beater. Pour into baked crust and bake 20-25 minutes at 350°. Bars are done when fairly firm. Chill. Cut into small squares and dust with powdered sugar. Rich and especially good for summer desserts and luncheons.

OATMEAL AND APPLE BUTTER BARS

1¼ cups flour
1 cup brown sugar, packed
¾ cup butter or margarine, cut up
1¼ cups quick-cooking oats
¾ cup apple butter

MAKES 16
Mix flour and sugar in large bowl. Cut in butter until mixture resembles coarse crumbs. (If you have a food processor, use it to mix flour, sugar, and butter.) Stir in oats until well mixed. Press half the mixture firmly in greased 8 inch square pan. Spread apple butter to within ½ inch of the edges. Sprinkle remaining oats mixture over apple butter; press carefully but firmly. Bake at 350° for 40 minutes or until lightly browned. Cool, and cut into 2 inch squares. These are simply scrumptious!

PRALINE BARS

1 pkg. graham crackers
2 sticks butter
1 cup light brown sugar
1 cup pecans, chopped

MAKES 24 BARS
Line the bottom of a lightly greased cookie pan (one with sides) with a layer of uncrushed graham crackers. Melt butter in small saucepan, and add 1 cup light brown sugar. Boil for 2 minutes. Remove from heat and add nuts. Pour and spread evenly over crackers. Bake 10 minutes at 350°. Cut while warm. These are extra easy and delicious, too.

PUMPKIN BARS

2 cups flour
1 tsp. soda
½ tsp. salt
1⅔ cup sugar
1 cup oil
4 eggs
2 cups pumpkin
1 cup nuts, chopped
2 tsp. baking powder
1 tsp. pumpkin pie spice or
    ¼ tsp. <u>each</u> cinnamon,
    allspice, cloves and
    nutmeg

FROSTING:
1—3 oz. pkg. cream cheese
¼ cup butter
2 Tbsp. cream
1 tsp. vanilla
2 cups powdered sugar

MAKES 4-5 DOZEN BARS
Mix all ingredients well. Pour into two greased and floured 9 x 13 inch pans and bake at 350° for 20-25 minutes.

To make frosting, mix together cream cheese and butter. Combine with other ingredients and mix well. Frost cooled bars. This big recipe makes a good holiday party treat.

 If you break an egg on the floor, sprinkle it heavily with salt and leave it alone for 5-10 minutes. Sweep the dried egg into a dustpan.

DESSERTS

SEVEN LAYER COOKIE

½ cup butter, melted
1 cup graham crackers,
    crushed
1 cup coconut
1 cup butterscotch chips,
    optional
1 cup chocolate chips
1 cup chopped nuts
1—15 oz. can sweetened
    condensed milk

MAKES 2 DOZEN

Combine melted butter with cracker crumbs in 9 x 13 inch pan. Press firmly into pan. Layer in order, the coconut, butterscotch chips, chocolate chips and nuts. Pour sweetened condensed milk evenly over all ingredients. Bake at 350° for 25-30 minutes.

FLAKY PIE CRUST

**ONE SINGLE 9 INCH PIE
CRUST:**
1⅓ cup flour
½ tsp. salt
½ cup Crisco
About 3-4 Tbsp. ice water

MAKES 9 INCH CRUST

Mix salt and flour with one hand. Add Crisco and break up shortening in flour until pieces are pea size. Sprinkle cold water over mixture and toss around with hand. Add enough water until dough holds together when gathered as if making a snowball. Avoid working the dough too much.

To make dough in a food processor, combine flour, salt and Crisco in processor. Blend until mealy. Add ice water, tablespoon at a time with machine running, until dough makes a ball.

Flatten dough on floured surface and roll about an inch larger than pan. Put in pan and trim edges. For a baked pie shell, bake at 450° for 8-10 minutes. (Be sure to prick the bottom and sides.)

 Make at least two pie crusts at a time. Freeze one in a pie pan and it will be ready for the next pie. You'll only have to clean up the mess once.

■♥■♥■♥■♥■♥■♥■♥■♥■♥■♥■♥■♥■♥■♥■♥■♥■

GRAHAM CRACKER CRUST

1 cellophane wrapped pkg.
  graham crackers (about
  20 crackers)
¼ cup sugar
⅓ cup butter, softened

MAKES ONE 9 INCH CRUST
Crush graham crackers in a food processor, or place in a plastic bag and crush them with a rolling pin. They should be finely crushed. Combine crumbs, sugar and butter and blend well. Press crumb mixture into 9-inch pie plate, covering the bottom and sides evenly. Bake at 375° for 8 minutes and cool.

MERINGUE

3 egg whites, room
  temperature
¼ tsp. cream of tartar
⅓ cup sugar

Beat egg whites and cream of tartar until foamy. Continue beating, gradually adding sugar. Beat until stiff. You can't overbeat. Spread onto hot or warm pie. Seal meringue to edge of crust. Bake 10 minutes at 375° or until golden brown.

A half of teaspoon of baking powder added to the room temperature egg whites before beating seems to "swell" the meringue and make it higher.

DESSERTS

AUNT GINGER'S APRICOT FRIED PIES

FILLING:
8 oz. dried apricots, diced
¼ cup cornstarch
1½ cups sugar
¼ tsp. salt
2 Tbsp. margarine

PASTRY:
4 cups flour
2 tsp. salt
1 cup shortening
¾-1 cup cold water

Crisco for frying

MAKES 12-15 PIES
Stew apricots in small amount of water until tender. Add sugar, salt, margarine and cornstarch and enough water to mix well. Cook several minutes, stirring constantly until thick. Chill fruit before making pies.

To prepare pastry, cut shortening into flour and salt until mealy. Add enough cold water to form pastry dough. Chill dough. Pull off a piece of dough about the size of a peach. Shape into a ball, roll out thin (pie crust thickness) on a floured board to a 6-inch round. Use a saucer as a guide to trim edges. Spoon fruit mixture not quite in the middle of the circle. Dampen edges of the rounds, fold over crust and mash edges together with fork or fingers on both sides. Prick a couple of holes on each side of the pie and fry in deep fat (2 inches of hot oil in a heavy skillet will work fine). These can be frozen before frying.

■♥■♥■♥■♥■♥■♥■♥■♥■♥■♥■♥■♥■♥■♥■

APPLE PIZZA PIE

1 ¼ cup flour
1 tsp. salt
½ cup shortening
1 cup cheddar cheese, grated
¼ cup ice water
½ cup powdered non-dairy creamer
½ cup brown sugar, packed
½ cup sugar
⅓ cup flour
¼ tsp. salt
1 tsp. cinnamon
½ tsp. nutmeg
¼ cup butter
2 Tbsp. lemon juice
6 cups peeled apple slices (½ inch thick)

SERVES 12

Mix 1 ¼ cup flour and salt; cut in shortening until crumbly. Add cheese. Sprinkle water over mixture and gradually shape into a ball. Roll pastry into 15 inch circle on floured surface. Place in pizza pan or large cast iron skillet and turn up edges. Combine non-dairy creamer, sugars, ⅓ cup flour, ¼ teaspoon salt and spices. Sprinkle half of mixture over pastry. Cut butter into remaining half until crumbly. Arrange apple slices, overlapping them in concentric circles on crust. Sprinkle with lemon juice and remaining crumbs. Bake at 450° for 30 minutes or until apples are tender. Serve warm.

DIXIE'S BUTTERMILK PIE

9-inch unbaked pie shell
1 ½ cups sugar
3 Tbsp. flour
2 eggs, well beaten
½ cup butter, melted
1 cup buttermilk
1 tsp. lemon extract
2 tsp. vanilla

SERVES 8

Combine sugar and flour; stir in eggs. Add melted butter and buttermilk, mix well. Stir in vanilla and lemon extract. Pour into chilled pie shell and bake at 425° for 10 minutes. Reduce heat to 350° and bake 35 additional minutes.

Use a regular size ice cream scoop when a recipe calls for one-quarter cup of shortening.

DESSERTS

COCONUT CREAM PIE

9 inch baked pie shell
⅔ cup sugar
¼ cup cornstarch
½ tsp. salt
3 cups milk
4 egg yolks
2 Tbsp. butter
2 tsp. vanilla
¾ cup flaked coconut

SERVES 8

In saucepan combine sugar, cornstarch and salt. Blend milk and egg yolks and add to sugar/cornstarch mixture. Cook over medium heat to boiling, stirring constantly. Boil 1 minute. Remove from heat, add vanilla, butter and coconut. Let cool; stirring occasionally. Pour into cooled pie shell. Top with meringue, sprinkle with coconut. Bake at 400° for 10 minutes or until light golden brown.

CHOCOLATE CREAM PIE

4 egg yolks
3 cups milk
1½ cups sugar
⅓ cup cornstarch
½ tsp. salt
2 oz. unsweetened
    chocolate
1 Tbsp. vanilla
9 inch baked pie shell

SERVES 8

In saucepan combine sugar, cornstarch and salt. Blend milk and egg yolks and add to sugar/cornstarch mixture. Cook over medium heat to boiling, stirring constantly. Boil 1 minute. Remove from heat, add vanilla and melted chocolate. Pour into baked pie shell and top with meringue. Bake at 400° for 10 minutes or until golden brown.

HERSHEY BAR PIE

9-inch graham cracker
crust
6 small chocolate almond
Hershey bars
16 large marshmallows
½ cup milk
1 cup whipping cream

SERVES 8
Melt candy bars, marshmallows and milk in double boiler. Cool thoroughly. Beat whipping cream until stiff. Fold into chocolate mixture. Pour into prepared graham cracker crust (a regular cooked pastry crust will work, too), and cover with plastic wrap. Refrigerate until serving time. Can be made ahead of time and kept in the freezer.

QUICK LEMON PIE

1 graham cracker crust
½ cup lemon juice (use
fresh lemons for better
results)
1 tsp. grated lemon rind
1⅓ cup sweetened
condensed milk
2 eggs, separated
1 Tbsp. sugar
¼ tsp. cream of tartar

SERVES 6
Combine lemon juice and lemon peel. Gradually stir in sweetened condensed milk. Add egg yolks, and stir until well blended. Pour into cooled graham cracker crust. Beat egg whites, adding cream of tartar and sugar gradually. Beat until almost stiff enough to hold a peak. Pile on pie. Bake at 325° until lightly browned, about 15 minutes. Let cool. If you prefer, you could mound Cool Whip on top (instead of meringue) and sprinkle slivered almonds to garnish.

Weeping meringue may be caused if any of the filling is exposed to the heat, (not entirely covered). Baking too long or incomplete blending of the sugar are also causes of weeping.

DESSERTS

OLD-FASHIONED LEMON PIE

9-inch baked pie shell
4½ Tbsp. flour
1 cup sugar
1¼ cups water
3 egg yolks
3 tsp. grated lemon rind
¼ cup lemon juice
2 Tbsp. butter

MERINGUE:
3 egg whites, room
    temperature
⅓ tsp. cream of tartar
6 Tbsp. sugar

SERVES 6-8
In top of double boiler, mix flour, sugar, water and egg yolks. Stir over boiling water until it begins to thicken. Put lid on pan and cook without stirring for 10 minutes. Remove from heat and add lemon rind, juice and butter. Mix well and pour into a baked pastry crust.

To make meringue, beat egg whites and cream of tartar, adding sugar gradually, until whites form stiff peaks. Top pie with meringue and bake 10 minutes at 375°.

LUCIOUS LAYERED PIE

1 cup flour
½ cup butter
¼ cup pecans, chopped
1—8 oz. pkg. cream cheese
1—12 oz. carton Cool Whip
1 cup powdered sugar
1 can pie filling (cherry,
    blueberry)
2 large boxes instant
    vanilla pudding
3 cups milk
2 Tbsp. lemon juice

SERVES 12
Combine flour, butter, and pecans in bowl and mix well. Press into 9 x 13 inch pyrex dish. Bake at 350° for 15 minutes. Cool. Combine softened cream cheese, 1 cup of Cool Whip and powdered sugar in bowl and mix well. Spread over cooled crust. Spread pie filling on top of cream cheese layer. To prepare fourth layer, combine instant pudding, milk and lemon juice in bowl and beat until stiff. Spread over pie filling. Top with remaining Cool Whip. Keep refrigerated.

DESSERTS

PECAN PIE

9-inch unbaked pie crust
3 eggs
½ cup sugar
¼ tsp. salt
1 cup light corn syrup
1⅓ cup pecans, broken or
   chopped
½ tsp. vanilla

SERVES 6-8
Beat eggs. Add other ingredients, mix well. Pour into pie shell. Bake 50 minutes at 325°.

FOURTH OF JULY STRAWBERRY PIE

9-inch baked pie crust
1—3 oz. pkg. cream cheese
½ cup powdered sugar
½ tsp. vanilla
1 pt. strawberries, whole or
   halved
½ cup strawberry juice (½
   cup strawberries blended
   with ¼ cup water)
⅔ cup sugar
2 Tbsp. cornstarch
1 cup whipping cream,
   whipped and sweetened

SERVES 6-8
Soften cream cheese and combine with powdered sugar and vanilla. Beat until smooth. Spread over bottom of cooled baked pie crust. Arrange whole or halved strawberries over bottom. Combine strawberry juice, sugar and cornstarch in saucepan. Mix well. Bring to boil stirring constantly. Simmer for ½ minute. Pour over strawberries in pie shell. Cool. Top each slice with whipped cream.

Egg whites are easier to beat if first warmed to room temperature.

197

DESSERTS

FRESH STRAWBERRY PIE

CRUST:
1 stick butter
2 Tbsp. sugar
1 cup flour

FILLING:
1½ pt. strawberries
1 cup water
1 cup sugar
3 Tbsp. cornstarch
2 Tbsp. strawberry jello
Whipped cream

SERVES 6-8
To prepare crust, melt butter and blend with sugar and flour. Press into pie pan. Bake at 350° for 15 minutes.

Slice 1 pint of strawberries and place in cooked pie shell. Puree water and ½ pint strawberries in blender. Combine strawberry juice, sugar and cornstarch in small saucepan. Mix well. Cook over medium heat until clear and thick. Add strawberry jello, mix well. Pour over berries while still warm. Chill several hours. Top with whipped cream.

SOUR CREAM RAISIN PIE

9-inch baked pie shell
1 cup buttermilk
1 cup sour cream
2 large egg yolks or 3
   small yolks, beaten
2 Tbsp. flour
1 Tbsp. cornstarch
¾ cup sugar
¾ cup raisins
¼ cup nuts, chopped big

SERVES 6-8
Combine all ingredients except raisins and nuts in large saucepan. Stir well before heating. Cook over medium heat, stirring constantly. Bring to boil and boil 1 minute. Add raisins and nuts. Put lid on pan and let sit 5-10 minutes. Pour into baked and cooled pie shell. Top with meringue, and bake at 400° about 10 minutes to brown. This pie is guaranteed to be a favorite. It comes highly recommended.

COFFEE CREME MOUSSE

1 lb. small marshmallows
1 cup very strong coffee
1 Tbsp. instant coffee
1 cup heavy cream,
   whipped
¼ tsp. almond extract

SERVES 6
In top of double boiler, melt marshmallows with coffee. Stir and cook until dissolved. Chill mixture until almost set. Fold in one cup heavy cream, whipped. Add almond extract. Pour into a lightly buttered ring mold (or any serving dish), and chill well. Invert and sprinkle top with toasted slivered almonds, or crushed nut brittle.

APPLE CRISP

6-8 medium cooking apples
   (about 6 cups sliced)
½ cup sifted flour
¾ cup firmly packed brown
   sugar
½ cup oats
¾ tsp. cinnamon
¾ tsp. nutmeg
⅓ cup butter or margarine

SERVES 8
Butter a 9x9x2 inch baking dish. Wash, pare, core, and thinly slice apples. Arrange in an even layer in baking dish. Set aside. Mix together flour, sugar, oats, and spices. In a food processor, if you have one, with a pastry blender if not, cut in the butter, until mixture is crumbly. Sprinkle flour, sugar, butter mixture over apples. Bake at 375° for 30 minutes or until crust is crisp and apples are tender. Serve warm, garnished with whipped cream or vanilla ice cream. This is a real treat to serve after a dinner of chili and green salad on the first cold night of the winter.

DESSERTS

FLAMING BANANA CREPES

12 dessert crepes
2 cups banana, chopped
1 Tbsp. lemon juice
½ cup shredded coconut, toasted
1 tsp. ground cinnamon

SAUCE:
2 Tbsp. butter
1 Tbsp. light corn syrup
1 pkg. Creamy White Frosting Mix (for single layer cake)
1 cup evaporated milk
¼ cup rum

SERVES 12

Toast coconut in oven until golden. Toss banana with lemon juice to coat. Mix with ¼ cup of coconut and cinnamon. Spoon filling along center of crepe and roll up.

To make sauce: Cook butter in saucepan until brown; remove from heat. Stir in corn syrup and frosting mix. Slowly stir in evaporated milk. Heat through, stirring constantly. Add sauce to crepes and sprinkle with remaining coconut. Heat until bubbly. Transfer to warm serving dish. Warm rum just until hot. Ignite; pour over crepes.

DESSERT CREPES:
2 eggs, beaten
⅓ cup milk
⅓ cup water
¾ cup flour
1 Tbsp. melted butter
2 Tbsp. sugar
1 tsp. vanilla

Add milk and water to beaten eggs in mixing bowl. Gradually add flour, stirring constantly with fork until mixture is smooth. Add remaining ingredients and beat until smooth. The batter should have the consistency of fresh cream. Pour thin layer in buttered skillet. Turn once. Brown lightly over medium heat on both sides, or cook on a crepe griddle.

 When beating egg whites, make sure the beater and bowl is completely free of fat or grease. (Don't use a plastic bowl.) A trace of grease can prevent the whites from getting stiff.

BANANA PUDDING

½ cup sugar
3 Tbsp. flour
Dash of salt
4 eggs, 3 of them
   separated
2 cups milk
½ tsp. vanilla
Box of vanilla wafers
5-6 medium ripe bananas

MERINGUE TOPPING:
3 egg whites
¼ cup sugar

SERVES 8

Combine ½ cup sugar, flour and salt in the top of double boiler. Mix in 1 whole egg and 3 egg yolks. Stir in milk. Cook, uncovered, stirring constantly until thickened. (Takes about 5 minutes . . . mixture should have the consistency of pudding.) Remove from heat and stir in vanilla. Spread about ¼ cupful on bottom of a 1½ quart casserole. Cover with layer of vanilla wafers, then layer of sliced bananas. Pour about ⅓ of the pudding over this layer, then continue layering wafers, bananas, and pudding until you have 3 layers of each, ending with pudding. Beat remaining 3 egg whites, gradually adding sugar until the mixture forms stiff peaks. Pile on top of pudding and bake at 425° for 5 minutes or until lightly browned.

CHEESE CAKE

Graham cracker crust,
   baked and cooled
12 oz. cream cheese
½ cup sugar
½ tsp. vanilla
2 eggs
1½ cups sour cream
2 Tbsp. sugar
½ tsp. vanilla

SERVES 6-8

Have ingredients at room temperature. Beat cream cheese, sugar, vanilla and eggs at moderate speed until smooth. Pour into graham cracker crust and bake at 325° for 20 minutes. Let cool 15 minutes. Spread with mixture of sour cream, sugar and vanilla. Return to oven for 5 minutes. Chill. Serve this plain, or with strawberries or blueberries poured over each piece. Either way you will get rave reviews.

DESSERTS

CHERRY CRUNCH

1—1 lb. 5 oz. can cherry
    pie filling
1 tsp. lemon juice
1 pkg. white cake mix
½ cup nuts, chopped
    (optional)
½ cup butter, melted

SERVES 8-10
Spread pie filling over bottom of a 9-inch square pan. Sprinkle with lemon juice. Combine cake mix, nuts and butter, sprinkle over pie filling. Place in preheated oven at 350° and bake for 45-50 minutes or until golden brown. Serve with ice cream or whipped cream.

PEACH COBBLER

4 cups fresh peaches,
    peeled and sliced
1 Tbsp. cornstarch
¼ cup water
½ cup sugar
¼ tsp. cinnamon

TOPPING:
½ cup flour
½ cup sugar
¼ tsp. salt
½ tsp. baking powder
1 egg
2 Tbsp. butter, melted

SERVES 6-8
Combine water and cornstarch in pan. Stir to dissolve cornstarch. Add fruit, sugar, and cinnamon. Cook until it thickens and boils. Pour into ungreased 2 quart baking dish. Combine flour, sugar, salt and baking powder. Mix together melted butter and egg and add to dry ingredients. Mix well with spoon. Drop spoonfuls of dough over fruit. Bake at 400° for 30-35 minutes or until brown. Other fruits can be substituted in this cobbler, by adjusting the sugar amounts for type of fruit.

SHERRI'S CREAM PUFFS

1 cup water
½ cup butter or margarine
1 cup flour
4 eggs

VANILLA CREAM FILLING:
½ cup sugar
3 Tbsp. cornstarch
¼ tsp. salt
2 cups milk
3 egg yolks
1 Tbsp. butter
1 Tbsp. vanilla

CHOCOLATE SAUCE:
½ cup sugar
4 tsp. cornstarch
½ cup water
1—1 oz. square
  unsweetened chocolate
Dash salt
1 Tbsp. butter
½ tsp. vanilla

MAKES 15
Combine water and butter in saucepan; bring to boil and stir until butter melts. Add flour all at once and stir constantly with wooden spoon until the mixture leaves the sides of the pan and forms a ball. Remove from heat. Immediately add unbeaten eggs one at a time, beating with mixer to a smooth paste after each one. Drop by heaping tablespoonfuls onto a greased baking sheet, about 3 inches apart. Bake in a hot oven (450°) for 15 minutes or until well puffed and delicately browned. Reduce heat to 300° and bake 20 minutes longer; this will bake the center thoroughly but puffs should get no browner. Remove to cake rack to cool. When cool, cut through center with a sharp knife. Fill with vanilla cream filling, whipped cream, ice cream or chocolate pudding. Replace tops and drizzle with chocolate sauce.

To make Cream Filling, combine sugar, cornstarch and salt in saucepan. Mix together milk and egg yolks and gradually stir into sugar mixture. Cook over medium heat, stirring constantly until mixture thickens and boils. Let boil 1 minute. Remove from heat, add butter and vanilla.

To prepare Chocolate Sauce, combine ½ cup sugar and cornstarch. Add water, chocolate and salt. Cook and stir until it thickens and bubbles. Remove from heat; stir in butter and vanilla.

Cream puffs are quick and easy to prepare, and if you're short on time, instant French Vanilla Pudding and warm Hershey's chocolate sauce can provide quick substitutes. This delicious dessert adds a real flair to a brunch.

DESSERTS

CAROL'S DATE PUDDING

1 cup dates, chopped
1 cup boiling water
½ cup white sugar
½ cup brown sugar
1 egg
2 Tbsp. melted oleo
1½ cup flour
½ tsp. salt
1 tsp. baking soda
½ tsp. baking powder
1½ cup brown sugar
1 Tbsp. butter
1½ cup boiling water

SERVES 12
Combine dates and boiling water. Mix and let cool. Mix white sugar, brown sugar, egg and melted oleo. Sift together flour, salt, baking soda, and baking powder; combine with sugar mixture. Mix well. Add dates. Pour into greased 11 x 7 inch pan (9 x 9 inch makes cake thicker). Combine the 1½ cups brown sugar, 1 tablespoon butter and 1½ cups boiling water. Pour over batter. Bake 40 minutes at 375°.

GINGERBREAD

2¼ cups flour
⅓ cup sugar
1 cup dark molasses
¾ cup hot water
½ cup shortening
1 egg
1 tsp. soda
1 tsp. ginger
1 tsp. cinnamon
½ tsp. salt

SERVES 12-16
Combine all ingredients in bowl. Mix well for three minutes. Pour into greased and floured 9 x 9 inch pan. Bake 40-50 minutes at 325°. Serve warm, topped with Lemon Sauce, whipped cream, or butter. What a treat on a cold winter night!

LEMON SAUCE:
½ cup sugar
4 tsp. cornstarch
Dash ground nutmeg
Dash salt
1 cup water
2 beaten egg yolks
2 Tbsp. butter
½ tsp. grated lemon peel
2 Tbsp. lemon juice

MAKES 1 CUP
In saucepan mix sugar, cornstarch, nutmeg, and dash salt. Gradually stir in 1 cup water. Cook and stir over low heat until thickened. Stir half the hot mixture into egg yolks; return to pan. Cook and stir 1 minute. Remove from heat; blend in remaining ingredients. Spoon over hot gingerbread.

PEACH MELBA

1 cup frozen raspberries
  and juice, thawed
1 tsp. sugar
1 tsp. cornstarch
4 large canned peach
  halves
Vanilla ice cream (or peach)

SERVES 4

Mix raspberries and juice, sugar, and cornstarch over low heat until clear. Strain and cool. Mound ice cream on each peach half, then pour sauce over top. This is an elegant, simple dessert. Serve it with shortbread cookies.

PEANUT BUTTER SAUCE

1 cup sugar
1 Tbsp. white corn syrup
¼ tsp. salt
¾ cup milk
6 Tbsp. peanut butter
¼ tsp. vanilla

MAKES 1 CUP

Mix sugar, corn syrup, salt, and milk and cook over low heat until thickened, stirring constantly. Add peanut butter and blend. Remove from heat and add vanilla when cool. Serve over vanilla or coffee ice cream.

RASPBERRY WALNUT TORTE

CRUST:
1 cup flour
⅓ cup powdered sugar
½ cup soft margarine

RASPBERRY LAYER:
1—10 oz. pkg. frozen
   raspberries
¾ cup walnuts, chopped
2 eggs
½ cup sugar
½ tsp. salt
½ tsp. baking powder
1 tsp. vanilla

SAUCE:
Liquid from raspberries
½ cup water
¼ cup sugar
2 Tbsp. cornstarch
2 drops red food coloring
2 Tbsp. lemon juice
½ cup raspberries
Whipped cream

SERVES 15
Combine 1 cup flour with powdered sugar and softened margarine. Press into 9 x 13 inch pan. Bake 15 minutes at 350°. Cool.

Drain raspberries, reserving juice and ½ cup raspberries for sauce. Spoon raspberries over crust. Sprinkle nuts on top of raspberries. In bowl, beat eggs with the sugar until light and fluffy. Add salt, baking powder and vanilla. Blend well. Pour over nuts and raspberries. Bake at 350° for 30-35 minutes until golden brown.

To prepare sauce, combine raspberry juice, ½ cup water, sugar, cornstarch and food coloring in small saucepan. Cook, stirring constantly until thick and clear. Add lemon juice and ½ cup raspberries.

To serve, cut squares of raspberry torte. Top with whipped cream and spoon sauce over top.

Use vegetable parer to make chocolate curls to decorate some desserts.

■♥■♥■♥■♥■♥■♥■♥■♥■♥■♥■■♥■♥■♥■♥■♥■♥■

STRAWBERRY SHORTCAKE

1 qt. fresh strawberries,
   sliced
1 cup sugar
2 cups flour
2 Tbsp. sugar
3 tsp. baking powder
1 tsp. salt
⅓ cup shortening
1 cup milk
Butter
Half and half or
   whipped cream

Slice strawberries, add sugar and mash gently. Let sit one-half hour. Combine flour, 2 tablespoons sugar, baking powder and salt in bowl. Cut in shortening until mixture is mealy. Stir in milk. Gather together and shape into four big "biscuits." Place in greased pan. Bake 15 minutes at 450° or until golden brown. Split shortcake while warm and spread with butter. Fill and top with strawberries. Serve warm with cream.

DESSERTS

PUMPKIN ROLL

4 eggs
1 cup sugar
1 tsp. lemon juice
⅔ cup pumpkin (canned)
1 cup flour
2 tsp. baking powder
1 tsp. ginger
1 tsp. nutmeg
2 tsp. cinnamon

FILLING:
4 Tbsp. butter, softened
6 oz. cream cheese,
   softened
1 cup powdered sugar
½ tsp. vanilla
1 cup nuts, chopped
Powdered sugar

SERVES 15

Beat eggs for about 3 minutes, then add sugar, lemon juice and pumpkin. Combine dry ingredients and fold into batter. Pour into greased jelly roll pan and bake for 15 minutes at 375°. While still warm, transfer cake onto a large tea towel and roll from narrow end. Allow to cool.

To prepare filling, cream butter and cream cheese. Add powdered sugar, vanilla, and nuts; mix well. When cake is cool, roll out and spread with filling. Roll back up (not in the towel), dust with powdered sugar, and slice to serve. Keep wrapped in plastic wrapping in the refrigerator. This is wonderful to have on hand during the holiday season.

DESSERT DELIGHT

1 cup flour
1 cup pecans, chopped
½ cup margarine
1—8 oz. pkg. cream cheese
1 cup powdered sugar
1—12 oz. carton Cool Whip
1 small pkg. instant
   chocolate pudding
1 small pkg. instant
   vanilla pudding
2 cups cold milk

SERVES 12

Mix together (in a food processor if you have one) flour, pecans and margarine—the mixture should resemble crumbs. Pat into 9 x 13 inch baking dish and bake 15 minutes at 350°. Let cool completely. Cream together cream cheese and powdered sugar. Stir in 1 cup Cool Whip and spread over cooled crust. Whip pudding mixes and milk together until thickened, and spread over cheese layer. Spread remaining Cool Whip on top. Chill before serving. This is a rich dessert, that looks like you worked really hard to put it together. In fact, it is a snap, and is always complimented.

CHOCOLATE MARENGO

24 chocolate wafers or
   12 Oreos
6 Tbsp. melted butter
4 egg whites
1/8 tsp. cream of tartar
1/4 cup sugar
Pinch salt
2 cups heavy cream
1 Tbsp. vanilla
6 oz. semi-sweet
   chocolate
1/2 cup slivered almonds,
   toasted

CHOCOLATE SAUCE:
1/2 cup sugar
4 tsp. cornstarch
1/2 cup water
1—1 oz. square
   unsweetened chocolate
Dash salt
1 Tbsp. butter
1/2 tsp. vanilla

SERVES 15

Crush wafers or Oreos and combine with melted butter. Press into 8 x 12 inch casserole dish. Bake at 350° for 8 minutes. Beat egg whites and cream of tartar. Gradually add sugar and salt and beat until stiff. In separate bowl, beat cream and vanilla until stiff. Fold cream into whites. Freeze in bowl until crystals form (1-1½ hours). Meanwhile, melt chocolate in double boiler or microwave. Toast almonds lightly in 300° oven and add to chocolate. Keep mixture hot. When frozen mixture is ready, fold chocolate into it. Streaks of chocolate will form. Pour into crust and freeze. Remove from freezer 20-30 minutes before serving. Pass chocolate sauce to be poured over each serving.

To prepare sauce, combine ½ cup sugar and cornstarch in small pan. Add water, chocolate and salt. Cook and stir until thickened and bubbly. Remove from heat; stir in butter and vanilla. This is an elegant dessert.

MUD PIE

1 chocolate cookie crust
   (in the cake mix section
   of your store)
1/2 gallon coffee ice cream,
   softened
Hershey's chocolate syrup
1—8 oz. carton Cool Whip
Slivered almonds

SERVES 8

Mound coffee ice cream in chocolate cookie crust. Generously drizzle chocolate syrup over ice cream. Pile Cool Whip on top of that, covering it to the edge like a meringue. Sprinkle slivered almonds on top of Cool Whip and freeze. Just before serving, take out of freezer and slice. This is a wonderfully rich dessert that takes about 5 minutes to put together. Your guests will be mightily impressed.

DESSERTS

OREO ICE CREAM

3 egg yolks
1—14 oz. can sweetened
   condensed milk
2 Tbsp. water
4 tsp. vanilla extract
1 cup coarsely crushed
   Oreo cookies
2 cups whipping cream,
   whipped

SERVES 10
Beat egg yolks in large bowl, stir in sweetened condensed milk, water and vanilla. Fold in cookies and whipped cream. Pour into 2 quart container. Cover and freeze 6 hours or until firm.

STRAWBERRY ICE CREAM

6 pts. fresh strawberries
2 cups sugar
1½ pts. whipping cream
1½ pts. half and half
1/8 tsp. salt

MAKES 4 QUARTS
Cover strawberries with sugar. Let stand an hour, stirring until syrup is formed. Mash. Add remaining ingredients and mix thoroughly. Pour into ice cream freezer container and proceed to freeze.

PEACH ICE CREAM

2½ cups sugar
14 large, ripe peaches,
   peeled and sliced
1/8 tsp. salt
Juice of 1 lemon
1½ pts. whipping cream
1½ pts. half and half
2 tsp. vanilla, optional
2 tsp. almond extract,
   optional

MAKES 4 QUARTS
Sprinkle sugar over peaches; let stand at least 1 hour, stirring occasionally until syrup is formed. Puree in food processor, or mash through a sieve or food mill. Add salt, lemon juice, whipping cream and half and half. Mix well. Pour into container of ice cream freezer and proceed with the freezing process.

HOMEMADE VANILLA ICE CREAM

6 eggs
3 cups sugar
2 Tbsp. vanilla
1½ qts. cream
Milk to fill freezer

Beat eggs until smooth. Add sugar, vanilla and 1 cup milk and beat well. Add remaining ingredients and mix well. Pour into ice cream freezer container and fill to freezer line with milk. Proceed to freeze.

VANILLA ICE CREAM

5 eggs
½ tsp. salt
1 Tbsp. vanilla
2½ cups sugar
1 qt. cream, or 1 large can
   evaporated milk
Milk

Beat eggs, salt and vanilla. Add sugar, beating as you pour. Pour in cream and mix well. Pour into ice cream freezer container and fill to the freeze line with milk. Stir well. Proceed to freeze.

DESSERTS

SINFULLY DELICIOUS DESSERT

24 Oreo sandwich
  cookies, crushed
⅓ cup butter, melted
1 qt. toasted almond ice
  cream
1 can evaporated milk
1—6 oz. pkg. semi-sweet
  chocolate pieces
½ small jar marshmallow
  creme
1 qt. coffee ice cream
1½ cups whipping cream,
  whipped
1½ oz. Kahlua liqueur
Powdered sugar
¼ cup toasted slivered
  almonds

SERVES 15-20
Combine melted butter with cookie crumbs. Press into buttered 9 x 13 inch pan. Bake at 350° for 8 minutes. When cooled, spoon softened almond ice cream over crust. Freeze until firm. In small saucepan, mix evaporated milk and chocolate pieces. Stir constantly over low heat until chocolate melts. Beat in marshmallow creme with a spoon. Cool. Spread over almond ice cream. Let sit in freezer until firm. Spread softened coffee ice cream over chocolate layer. Sprinkle toasted almonds over coffee ice cream. Whip cream, adding powdered sugar to taste and Kahlua. Spread over coffee layer. Garnish with chocolate curls. Freeze. Let sit out 20-30 minutes before serving.

RUTH'S FROSTY STRAWBERRY SQUARES

CRUST:
1 cup flour
¼ cup brown sugar
½ cup softened margarine
½ cup chopped walnuts

TOPPING:
2 egg whites
½ cup sugar
2 Tbsp. lemon juice
1 large container frozen
  strawberries, sliced
½ pt. whipping cream,
  whipped

SERVES 15-20
Stir crust ingredients together. Remove ½ cup mixture to be used for topping. Press remaining crust mixture into 9 x 13 inch pan. Bake 15-20 minutes at 350°. Also bake the ½ cup of crumbs in a pie pan; stir occasionally. Beat egg whites, gradually adding sugar and lemon juice. When whites begin to stiffen, gradually add strawberries, beating mixture until stiff—about 15 minutes. Fold in ½ pint whipped cream. Pour on top of cooled crust. Top with remaining crumbs. Cover and freeze. Delicious luncheon or summertime dessert.

ALICE'S NUT GOODIE BARS

1—12 oz. pkg. butterscotch
   chips
1—12 oz. pkg. chocolate
   chips
1 cup chunky peanut butter
1 cup salted peanuts (dry
   roasted can be used)
1—10½ pkg. miniature
   marshmallows

Melt all chips together. Add peanut butter. Stir in nuts and marshmallows. Pour into buttered 9 x 13 inch pan. Cut into candy size pieces.

PECAN MILLIONAIRES

1 pkg. Kraft's caramels
2-3 tsp. water
1½ cups whole pecans
8 Hershey bars, plain
¼ bar paraffin

MAKES 2 DOZEN
Melt caramels with water. Add the pecans. Spoon out on greased wax paper and let cool. Melt Hershey bars and paraffin in double boiler. Dip caramel candies into chocolate mixture and place back on waxed paper to set.

FREDA'S PEANUT BRITTLE

1 cup sugar
½ cup white corn syrup
1 cup raw peanuts
½ tsp. vanilla
3 Tbsp. butter
1 tsp. soda

Combine sugar, syrup and peanuts in a large cast iron skillet. Cook over high heat until sugar turns a rich golden color. Add vanilla and butter to candy. Stir fast, until butter melts. Add soda and and stir very fast. Pour immediately onto a sheet of aluminum foil or buttered cookie sheet. Let harden, then break into pieces with the handle of a knife. The last part of the recipe goes very fast. . . you should have the butter, vanilla, and soda premeasured and ready to add when it's time. Wash the skillet immediately to make clean-up easier.

DESSERTS

MOM'S CARAMEL POPCORN

2 gal. popped popcorn
2 cups brown sugar
2 sticks butter
½ cup white corn syrup
1 tsp. soda
1 tsp. salt

MAKES 2 GALLONS
Combine brown sugar, butter, syrup and salt in saucepan. Heat to boiling, continue to boil 5 minutes, stirring occasionally. Remove from heat, add soda. Mix well. Pour over popped corn, mixing well. Put into 2 large pans. Bake in 200° oven for 1 hour. Stir every 15 minutes.

FUDGE

4 cups sugar
1 stick margarine
1 large can evaporated milk
1—12 oz. pkg. chocolate chips
1 small jar marshmallow creme
1 cup chopped pecans
1 tsp. vanilla

MAKES 2-3 DOZEN
Combine sugar, margarine, and milk in saucepan. Bring to boil. Stir 5 minutes over medium heat to soft ball stage (235° on candy thermometer). Remove from heat, stir in chocolate chips. Add marshmallow creme, nuts, and vanilla. Heat until well blended. Pour into greased pan. Cool. Cut into squares.

PARTY MINTS

1 lb. powdered sugar
¼ cup butter
4 Tbsp. cream
Flavoring of your choice: vanilla, almond, peppermint, orange, lemon to taste
Coloring

MAKES 4-5 DOZEN
Soften butter and combine with sugar and cream. Add flavoring and coloring. Knead well. Press into forms.

PRALINES

1 cup brown sugar
1 cup sugar
½ tsp. soda
1/8 tsp. salt
¾ cup buttermilk
Dash of cream of tartar
2 cups pecans
2 Tbsp. butter
1½ tsp. vanilla

MAKES 2 DOZEN
Cook sugars, soda, salt, buttermilk and cream of tartar to softball stage (234° on candy thermometer). Add pecans and butter and cook just a minute more. Remove from heat. Add vanilla. Cool slightly and beat until creamy, but still not too thick. At this point, you must hurry, dropping them by spoonfuls on wax paper, so they do not harden before you spoon them out. These are sure to be a favorite!

ENGLISH TOFFEE

1 cup pecans, chopped
¾ cup brown sugar
½ cup butter
½ cup chocolate chips

Butter a 9 x 9 inch dish. Spread chopped pecans over bottom of dish. Heat sugar and butter to boiling, stirring constantly. Boil over medium heat for 7 minutes. Spread mixture evenly over nuts in pan. Spread with knife to flatten. Sprinkle chocolate pieces over the hot candy. When melted, spread with knife. Cut into squares while hot or break into pieces when cool. A rainy or humid day may affect the success of this recipe.

Candies cook best in dry cool weather. Always use a wooden spoon to stir the candy, as it will help prevent crystalizing.

Preserves,
Relishes
&
Sauces

PRESERVES, RELISHES & SAUCES

BLUEBERRY-ORANGE MARMALADE

1 medium orange
1 lime or lemon
⅔ cup water
2 pints blueberries
5 cups sugar
½ bottle liquid pectin

MAKES 4 PINTS

Shred or grate orange and lime (or lemon) peel. Combine water and peel in kettle, heat to boiling. Reduce heat, cover and simmer 10 minutes, stirring occasionally. Wash blueberries, drain and mash. Cut white portion off orange and lemon and puree remaining fruit pulp in a blender. Add pulp to cooked peel mixture along with blueberries. Heat fruit mixture to boiling. Reduce heat, cover and simmer 10 minutes. Stir in sugar and heat to full rolling boil, stirring constantly. Stir in pectin, heat again to full rolling boil. Boil hard for 1 minute, stirring constantly. Remove from heat, skim. Ladle into hot jars and adjust lids. Process in boiling water bath 10 minutes.

FRANCES' JALAPENO PEPPER JELLY

¾ lb. bell pepper (2 cups) seeded, and chopped
½ lb. jalapeno peppers, fresh, or 1½ cups seeded, canned hot peppers
6½ cups sugar
1½ cups apple cider vinegar
1—6 oz. bottle liquid pectin

MAKES 4 PINTS

Remove all seeds from peppers before grinding. Grind peppers finely and add to sugar and vinegar. Save juice from ground peppers. Bring peppers, sugar and vinegar to boil and boil for 4-5 minutes. Add bottle of pectin and juice from peppers. Boil for 3 minutes. Pour into sterilized jars and seal with paraffin. This is delicious as a condiment with meat, or great with cheese and crackers. Wear gloves while preparing peppers, or your hands will burn.

PRESERVES. RELISHES & SAUCES

CHOKECHERRY JELLY

3 cups chokecherry juice
6½ cups sugar
1 bottle liquid fruit pectin

MAKES 5 PINTS

To prepare juice, place 3½ pounds chokecherries with 3 cups water in large kettle. Cover and cook 15 minutes. Place in jelly bag and squeeze out juice. Pour juice in large kettle, add sugar and stir. Bring to boil stirring constantly. Stir in pectin, bring to full rolling boil and boil hard 1 minute, stirring constantly. Remove from heat, stir, and skim for 5 minutes. Pour into hot glasses. Cover with paraffin or adjust lids and process in boiling water bath 5 minutes.

This jelly is truly a Colorado native. Chokecherry bushes flourish along the roadsides and grassland areas of the front range, providing those of us lucky enough to discover them before the birds do, a batch of beautiful purple berries just right for making this delicious jelly!

PEACH PRESERVES

1 lb. prepared peaches
¾-1 lb. sugar

MAKES 6 PINTS

To prepare fruit, select peaches at firm, ripe stage. Wash and pare the peaches. Cut into pieces and combine sugar and fruit in alternate layers in a container. Mixture can stand 8-10 hours, overnight, or add the sugar and ¼ cup water for each pound of fruit and cook at once. Stir carefully while heating to a boil. Cook until thick. Fill hot dry jars to ½ inch from top. Seal with paraffin.

PRESERVES, RELISHES & SAUCES

STRAWBERRY JAM

1 qt. strawberries
3 Tbsp. lemon juice
1 qt. sugar

MAKES 2 PINTS
Combine strawberries and lemon juice in kettle. Boil 3 minutes. Add sugar and bring to rolling boil. Boil 9 minutes. Pour into shallow pan. Skim off foam. Lay clean tea towel or cheesecloth over top of pan. Let set, stirring occasionally for 24 hours. Pour into sterilized jars and seal with wax.

CHILI SAUCE

4 qts. ripe tomatoes,
   peeled and chopped
1 cup white onion,
   finely ground
1 cup green pepper,
   finely ground
1 cup sweet red peppers,
   finely ground
2 cups sugar
2 Tbsp. salt
¼ tsp. cayenne pepper
1 Tbsp. whole cloves
3—3 inch sticks whole
   cinnamon
1 Tbsp. mustard seed
3 cups vinegar

MAKES 5 PINTS
Wash vegetables thoroughly. Remove seeds and white portions from peppers before chopping. Combine vegetables, sugar, salt and cayenne in heavy pan. Place over low heat and stir until sugar is dissolved. Cook slowly, stirring occasionally, about 2 hours or until mixture thickens. Add spices, tied in a square of cheesecloth, and vinegar. Cook, stirring occasionally until very thick, about 30 minutes. Remove cheesecloth bag. Pour immediately into hot sterilized jars. Adjust lids and process in boiling water bath 15 minutes. Good on roast beef or hamburgers.

 A simple way to handle the melting of paraffin is to have a permanent paraffin cup or small coffee can in which paraffin is always kept. While jellying, put the cup in a pan of water over low heat. Add new paraffin as needed. When jelly making is completed, let the paraffin harden in the cup. Put in a plastic bag and store with canning equipment.

PRESERVES, RELISHES & SAUCES

CHUTNEY

12 medium apples,
  unpeeled and diced
6 medium green tomatoes,
  diced
1 cup onion, chopped
1 cup green pepper,
  chopped
1 lb. raisins
1 qt. cider vinegar
3 cups brown sugar
3 Tbsp. mustard seed
2 Tbsp. ground ginger
2 tsp. salt
2 tsp. allspice

MAKES 10 PINTS
Combine all ingredients in large kettle. Simmer slowly for 1-1½ hours or until thick. Stir frequently and watch closely at end as it burns easily. Ladle into hot jars; adjust lids. Process in boiling water bath 5 minutes. This is exceptional poured over a brick of cream cheese and served as an appetizer with crackers. Also good on turkey or chicken sandwiches.

POOSE'S CHOW-CHOW

2 large heads cabbage
  (about 8 lbs.)
¼ bushel green tomatoes
  (about 12 lbs.)
6-7 large bell peppers
5-6 large onions
1 cup (or more if you
  prefer) hot green peppers
1 gal. vinegar (white)
5 cups sugar
½ cup salt
1 tsp. allspice
1 tsp. celery seed
1 tsp. alum
1 tsp. turmeric
1 Tbsp. dry mustard
2 Tbsp. pickling spices
½ tsp. ground cloves

MAKES 15-20 PINTS
Grind first five ingredients. Place on a large dish towel and sprinkle with salt. Tie corners of towel together to make a bag. Let stand in the sink for about 2 hours. Tie pickling spices in a cheesecloth bag. Put the bagged spices in bottom of large Dutch oven, and add all other ingredients. If necessary, add enough water to cover the vegetables. Cook about 25 minutes, stirring occasionally. Keep chow-chow at near boiling while filling the hot sterilized jars. Adjust lids and process in boiling water bath 15 minutes. This is a great relish for hot dogs, roast beef, tuna fish, and especially dabbed on top of Cowboy Beans!

Always wear rubber gloves when working with jalapeno peppers or hot chili peppers. The juice from the peppers will burn your hands.

PRESERVES, RELISHES & SAUCES

GREEN TOMATO RELISH

½ bushel green tomatoes
   (48-56 medium)
12 green bell peppers,
   seeded
12 red bell peppers,
   seeded
6-8 white onions
2 qts. cider vinegar
1 qt. white vinegar
7 cups sugar
½ cup salt
1 cup mustard seed (10 oz.)
3 Tbsp. celery seed
1 Tbsp. cinnamon
1 Tbsp. allspice

MAKES 15-20 PINTS
Grind the vegetables together. A food processor works great. Drain off liquid, using a collander. Put vegetables in large kettle. Add 2 quarts vinegar. Boil 30 minutes, stirring frequently. Drain very well. Add 1 quart vinegar, sugar, salt, and spices. Simmer 3 minutes, pack in hot jars, adjust lids and process in boiling water bath 15 minutes. This is very good on roast beef, but serves the purpose of any good relish. Makes great Christmas presents!

ZUCCHINI RELISH

10 cups finely chopped
   zucchini (can also be
   grated)
4 cups finely chopped
   onion
2 green peppers, chopped
2 red peppers, chopped
   (or 1 jar pimentos)
⅓ cup salt
¼ tsp. turmeric
1 tsp. nutmeg
1 tsp. celery seed
1 tsp. pepper
1 Tbsp. cornstarch
2½ cups vinegar
4½ cups sugar

MAKES 6 PINTS
Combine zucchini, onion, green pepper, red pepper and salt in large cooker or canner. Mix well and let stand overnight. Drain and rinse well with cold water. Add remaining ingredients and boil 20-30 minutes. Ladle into hot jars and adjust lids. Process in boiling water bath 15 minutes.

PICKLED BEETS

2 cups sugar
2 cups water
2 cups vinegar
1 tsp. cloves
1 tsp. allspice
1 Tbsp. cinnamon
15-20 small to medium
   beets

MAKES 5 PINTS
Remove beet tops, leaving roots and about 1 inch of stem. Cover with boiling water and cook until tender. Remove skins and slice beets. The small beets can be pickled whole or can be chunked. Combine liquid, sugar, and spices. Heat to boiling. Add beets and simmer 5 minutes. Pack beets and juice into hot jars. Adjust lids. Process in boiling water bath 30 minutes.

BREAD 'N BUTTER PICKLES

4 qts. cucumbers, sliced
⅓ cup salt
6 medium onions, sliced
   (6 cups)
2 green peppers,
   chopped (1⅔ cup)
3 cloves garlic
3 cups cider vinegar
5 cups sugar
1½ tsp. celery seed
2 Tbsp. mustard seed
1½ tsp. turmeric

MAKES 8 PINTS
Combine cucumbers, onion, green pepper and garlic cloves. Add salt and mix gently. Cover with ice, mix well and let stand 3 hours. Drain well, and remove garlic. Combine remaining ingredients in a large kettle. Boil 10 minutes. Add cucumber mixture to liquid and bring to boiling point. Pack loosely in hot jars; adjust lids. Process in boiling water bath 15 minutes. Note: If you have ½ bushel of cucumbers to pickle, you must quadruple (4x) this recipe.

PRESERVES, RELISHES & SAUCES

CONWAY SPRINGS DILL PICKLES

¼ bushel pickling
  cucumbers
Fresh dill
1 qt. white vinegar
2 qts. water
¾ cup pickling salt
1 Tbsp. alum

MAKES 10 QUARTS
Slice clean cucumbers lengthwise or leave smaller ones whole. Combine vinegar, water, salt, and alum; heat to boiling. Place 3-4 heads of fresh dill in the bottom of clean, hot sterilized jar. Pack pickles standing, tightly as possible, adding 2-3 heads of fresh dill on top. Pour the boiling hot vinegar mixture to cover. Adjust lids and process in boiling water bath 10 minutes. If pickling a few jars at a time, as cucumbers ripen, save the vinegar mixture and reheat it for the next batch. To get a good dill flavor in these pickles, don't open them for at least six weeks after canning.

HOMEMADE V-8 JUICE

7 cups water
½ bushel of tomatoes
1 red beet, peeled and
  quartered
2 carrots, cut in quarters
1 green pepper, quartered
6 onions, quartered
4 Tbsp. salt
¾ cup sugar
¼ cup lemon juice
6 stalks celery
¼ cup vinegar

MAKES 4 QUARTS
Combine all ingredients in large kettle. Let simmer for 2 hours. Run mixture through juicer. Heat juice to boiling and ladle into hot jars; adjust lids. Process in boiling bath 10 minutes.

PRESERVES, RELISHES & SAUCES

CREAM CHEESE SAUCE

½ cup milk
8 oz. cream cheese
¼ cup Parmesan cheese
½ Tbsp. onion salt

MAKES 1½ CUPS
Warm milk in saucepan. Add cubed cream cheese. Let melt, stirring often. Add Parmesan cheese and onion salt. Delicious on asparagus.

HOLLANDAISE SAUCE

2 egg yolks
2½-3 Tbsp. lemon juice
½ cup cold butter

MAKES 1 CUP
Combine egg yolk and lemon juice in small saucepan. Mix briskly. Add cube of butter whole, do not cut up. Stir over low heat until thickened. Serve immediately. If it looks curdled instead of creamy and smooth, beat vigorously over low heat again.

STEAK BUTTER

1 pint sour cream
1 carton (8 oz.) whipped
    butter
2-3 Tbsp. minced parsley
¼ tsp. garlic powder
2 Tbsp. chives, chopped
Salt and pepper

MAKES 2 CUPS
Mix all ingredients thoroughly and refrigerate. Remove from refrigerator at least 1 hour before serving. This can be frozen and re-frozen easily. If frozen, let thaw and whip before using. To use, plop one or more tablespoons over steaks while they are hot. Also good on baked potatoes.

PRESERVES, RELISHES & SAUCES

HICKORY BARBECUE SAUCE

1—20 oz. bottle ketchup
½ cup water
¼ cup cider vinegar
1 Tbsp. packed brown
  sugar
1 Tbsp. Worcestershire
  sauce
1 tsp. salt
1 tsp. onion powder
½ tsp. liquid smoke
1/8 tsp. garlic powder

MAKES 3 CUPS
Blend all ingredients in blender or food processor until smooth. Store in refrigerator. Use on ribs, chicken, pork chops, or beef brisket. Also good on sandwiches. Keep this on hand.

TARTAR SAUCE

1 cup mayonnaise
¼ cup dill pickles, chopped
1 Tbsp. chopped pimento
2 Tbsp. grated onion
2 tsp. vinegar
1 tsp. sugar
½ tsp. Tabasco

MAKES 1½ CUPS
Combine all ingredients. Mix well and refrigerate. Serve with fish.

JEZEBEL SAUCE

1—6 oz. jar prepared
  mustard
1—6 oz. jar prepared
  horseradish
1—8 oz. or 10 oz. jar apple
  jelly
1—8 oz. or 10 oz. jar
  pineapple preserves

Mix all ingredients together. No cooking necessary. This sauce is especially good with ham, or poured over cream cheese and served with crackers as an appetizer. Makes a really nice gift, too.

PRESERVES, RELISHES & SAUCES

THE NEIGHBORS' SAUCY HAM SAUCE

1 cup sour cream
1 Tbsp. horseradish
2 Tbsp. prepared mustard

Add horseradish and mustard to sour cream. So good with ham!

BRANDIED MUSHROOM SAUCE

1 cup whipping cream
3 Tbsp. butter or margarine
2 green onions, chopped
2 cups sliced, fresh
   mushrooms
2 Tbsp. brandy
Salt
Pepper

MAKES 2 CUPS
In a small pan bring unwhipped cream to boil. Stirring constantly, continue to boil about 5 minutes until cream thickens. Remove from heat. Melt butter. Add onions and saute a few minutes until onions are transparent. Add mushrooms. Cook over moderate heat about 4 minutes, stirring constantly. Add brandy and cream. Mix lightly but thoroughly. Add salt and pepper to taste. Heat to serving temperature. Serve as a sauce with sliced, roast turkey or Cornish hens.

Kids'
Food

SILLY SALLY SALAD

Body . . . . canned peach half
Arms and legs . . . . small celery sticks
Head . . . . half of a hard cooked egg
Eyes, nose, shoes, buttons . . . . raisins
Mouth . . . . red hot cinnamon candy
Hair . . . . grated yellow cheese
Skirt . . . . piece of lettuce

CELERY BOATS

Celery stalks
Peanut butter
Cream cheese
Pimento cheese
Raisins
Nuts

Clean celery stalks and cut into 2-3 inch lengths. Spread the filling of your choice into each. Top with raisins or nuts.

SUPERMAN STEAK

Make a beef patty, using lean ground beef. Broil, pan fry or grill outside. When done, add cheese and ketchup to make the "Superman" logo. You will be the "Super Hero" with your kids!!!

COTTONTAIL SALAD

1 chilled pear half
Raisins
1 red hot candy
2 blanched almonds
1 tsp. cottage cheese
2 toothpicks, broken
   in half
Lettuce leaves

Place pear center-down on a bed of lettuce. Add raisins for eyes, red hot for nose, toothpicks for whiskers, almonds for ears, and cottage cheese for tail.

PLUM DELICIOUS CASSEROLE

1 lb. ground beef
1 can cream of chicken
   soup
½ can water
1—16 oz. pkg. frozen
   Tater Tots

Brown ground beef. Drain fat. Place in large casserole. Cover with cream of chicken soup, diluted with ½ can water. Place frozen Tater Tots over top and bake uncovered at 350° for 1 hour. Kids like to make and eat this recipe.

SANDWICH IDEAS

Spread 2 slices of bread with butter or cream cheese. Using a cookie cutter, cut each sandwich into shapes. On Valentine's Day, tint the cream cheese with red food coloring, cut each sandwich into the shape of a heart.

Puree peanut butter and banana together, spread on two pieces of bread. Cut sandwich into quarters. Surprise each child with an animal cracker riding atop his sandwich!

PIGS IN THE BLANKET

Pork sausage links or
   hot dogs
Refrigerated prepared
   biscuits

Brown sausage or hot dogs. Drain and cool. Roll each biscuit flat, then wrap around sausage. Bake on a cookie sheet at 450° for 10-12 minutes.

 Hairspray removes ballpoint ink. Spray it directly on the surface then wipe away with warm sudsy water.

KIDS' FOOD

ONE MINUTE DONUTS

1 tube of refrigerator
  biscuits
Oil for cooking
Frosting or sugar

MAKES 10
Heat oil to 375°. Poke hole in center of biscuit. Deep fry to a golden brown on both sides. Roll in sugar or frost. Quick and easy. Great breakfast treat for kids.

FRENCH TOAST

1 egg
½ tsp. sugar
1 slice bread

SERVES 1
With fork, beat egg and sugar in pie pan. Dip bread in egg to coat both sides well. Fry in buttered skillet over medium-low heat to lightly brown both sides. Top with butter, powdered sugar, and pancake syrup.

BULL'S EYE EGGS

1 slice bread
1 egg
Butter

SERVES 1
Cut out center of a slice of bread with a biscuit cutter. Butter bread on both sides, then brown one side of bread in moderately hot buttered frying pan. Turn over, then drop egg in center of toast. Cook slowly until egg white is set.

234

SHERBET FLOAT

Put 1-2 scoops sherbet (your choice of flavors, orange is good) in a tall glass. Pour 7-Up to cover.

STRAWBERRY SODA

Put 2 scoops vanilla ice cream in a tall glass. Pour in strawberry soda to cover.

BOB'S CHOCOLATE SODA

2 Tbsp. chocolate syrup
¼ cup club soda
1-2 large scoops vanilla
   ice cream
¼ cup club soda

SERVES 1
Mix syrup and club soda in a tall glass. Add ice cream. Pour in more soda. Stir to blend and serve at once.

SPARKLING FRUIT PUNCH

2 pkgs. strawberry Koolaid
2 cups sugar
1 can frozen orange juice
   concentrate
1 can frozen lemonade
   concentrate
3-4 qts. water
1 pint ginger ale

Mix ingredients and add 1 pint ginger ale just before serving. Can also use lime Koolaid.

YOGURT SUNDAE

Yogurt (your choice of flavor)
Fresh fruit
Honey
Nuts
Maraschino cherry

Freeze the yogurt. Scoop out into an ice cream dish. Add fresh fruit, then honey. Sprinkle with nuts. Top with a maraschino cherry.

ICE CREAM CLOWNS

Place a round scoop ice cream on a piece of cake. Put an ice cream cone upside down on top of the ice cream for a hat. Make a face with cherries, pecan halves for ears, and decorate hat with whipped cream rosettes.

PARTY ICE CREAM CONE CAKES

1 Jiffy cake mix, any flavor
12-15 ice cream cones
Frosting

MAKES 12-15
Prepare cake as directed on the box. Spoon batter into cones ½-¾ full. Bake at 350° for 15 minutes or until done. Frost and decorate to fit the occasion.

RAINBOW ICE

Freeze cranberry juice, grape juice, orange juice or left-over juices and syrups from canned fruits in ice cube trays. Sparkle up your lemonade with these ice cube treats!

POPCORN BALLS

40 large marshmallows
¼ cup butter
5 cups popped popcorn
Food coloring, optional

MAKES 1 DOZEN
Melt marshmallows and butter over low heat. Add food coloring and mix well. Pour popped corn in large bowl or roasting pan. Pour marshmallow mixture over popcorn while stirring. Mix well to coat all of the corn. Butter your hands and form popcorn mixture into balls.

PUDDING POPS

Combine 1 large package instant pudding with 3 cups of milk. Mix only enough to blend well. Quickly pour into popsicle molds and freeze.

WHITE CHOCOLATE PRETZELS

1 pkg. vanilla flavored
Candiquik
1 pkg. pretzels

Melt Candiquik in top of double boiler. (Water must be very hot, but not boiling). Remove from heat when melted and dip pretzels in to cover. Set on waxed paper until cool.

S'MORES

Graham crackers
Marshmallows
Hershey's chocolate bars

Set 4 squares of candy bar on a graham cracker. Toast a marshmallow, then slip it on chocolate and top with a second graham cracker. Eat like a sandwich. You'll be sure to want s'more!

HAYSTACKS

1 cup chow mein noodles
1—6 oz. pkg. butterscotch
chips (may substitute
chocolate chips)
½ cup chopped nuts or
salted peanuts

MAKES 15
Melt chips in microwave or in top of a double boiler. Remove from heat and stir in noodles and nuts. Mix well and drop by teaspoonfuls on greased cookie sheet or waxed paper. Let stand until firm.

TRAIL MIX SNACK

1—15 oz. box seedless
raisins
1—12 oz. can Spanish
peanuts
1—12 oz. pkg. milk
chocolate chips (may
substitute carob chips)

Mix the ingredients together for a high energy, nutritious snack.

E.T. COOKIES

1 cup sugar
1 cup light corn syrup
1 cup peanut butter
5 cups Rice Krispies

ICING:
1—6 oz. pkg. chocolate
   chips
½ cup powdered sugar
2 Tbsp. butter
1 Tbsp. water

MAKES 2 DOZEN
Boil 1 minute the sugar, corn syrup and peanut butter. Stir in Rice Krispies, then press into a buttered 9 x 13 inch pan. Melt chocolate chips in small saucepan with butter and water. Combine with powdered sugar and mix well. Spread on top of Rice Krispies. Cut into squares.

ONE-PAN GRAHAM-BANANA SQUARES

1¼ cups graham cracker
   crumbs
½ cup wheat germ
2 Tbsp. packed brown
   sugar
½ tsp. baking soda
Dash of salt
1 cup mashed bananas
   (2 medium)
⅓ cup peanut butter
2 Tbsp. oil
1 cup semi-sweet chocolate
   chips

MAKES 16
In a 9-inch square baking pan, mix crumbs, wheat germ, sugar, soda and salt. Add bananas, peanut butter, and oil which have been blended together (a food processor will do the trick). Mix until thoroughly blended, using a fork, spatula or your fingers. The dough will be thick. Press evenly into the pan, sprinkle with chocolate chips, and bake at 350° for 30 minutes. Cool and cut in 2-inch squares. This cookie is highly nutritious, easy for kids to make, and an all time favorite.

Spray your measuring cup with Pam before measuring corn syrup—it will all pour out easily.

KIDS' FOOD

DOUG'S CHEESEY PRETZELS

1½ cups flour
⅔ cup milk
½ cup cheddar cheese,
  shredded
2 Tbsp. butter or margarine
2 tsp. baking powder
1 tsp. sugar
1 tsp. salt
1 egg, beaten
Coarse salt, onion salt, or
  garlic salt

MAKES 16
Beat first seven ingredients with a fork until well mixed. Divide dough into 16 parts. Make "snakes" with your hands, then form into pretzel shapes or whatever shape you like. Lay carefully on a greased cookie sheet, brush with beaten egg, sprinkle lightly with salt, and bake at 400° for 20 minutes or until golden brown. This is a yummy and nutritious "snake-up" snack. Easy and fun for kids to make and eat!

CHRISTMAS WREATHS

¼ cup butter
1—16 oz. pkg. marsh-
  mallows (40 large
  marshmallows)
5 cups corn flakes
Green food coloring
Cinnamon candies

MAKES 2 DOZEN
Melt butter and marshmallows in large saucepan over low heat, stirring constantly. Remove from heat. Add green food coloring. Mix well. Add corn flakes, mix with melted marshmallows. Shape into small wreaths on wax paper. Place several hot cinnamon candies on wreath for decoration.

GINGER COOKIE DOUGH
(for Gingerbread Men)

1 cup shortening
1 cup brown sugar, packed
1 Tbsp. cinnamon
1 Tbsp. ginger
1 cup dark corn syrup
2 eggs
5½ cups flour
1½ tsp. baking soda

ICING:
2 cups powdered sugar
½ tsp. vanilla
2 Tbsp. milk

In a large bowl, cream shortening with brown sugar, cinnamon and ginger until fluffy. Beat in corn syrup and eggs until well-blended. Mix 2 cups flour with baking soda; beat into creamed mixture. Stir in remaining 3½ cups flour, working with hands if necessary to get a smooth dough. Wrap airtight; chill overnight. Roll chilled dough to ¼ inch thickness and cut into desired shapes. Decorate with raisins or red hots, and bake at 375° for 10 minutes. Ice when cooled.

Mix all icing ingredients until smooth and of desired consistency. You can color the icing at this point, or put it in a decorator's tube to outline the gingerbread boys.

JACK-O-LANTERN PIZZAS

4 English muffins, split
1 Tbsp. vegetable oil
1—8 oz. can pizza sauce
8 slices (3½ x 3½ in.)
mozzarella cheese

MAKES 8

Place split muffins on a baking sheet. Brush top of each muffin with a little oil. Broil muffins until they are light brown. Remove from oven. Measure one generous tablespoonful of pizza sauce onto each muffin. Spread evenly. Trim corners from cheese slices to make circles. Cut out a jack-o'-lantern face on each circle with a paring knife. Place 1 cheese face on each pizza muffin. Bake pizzas at 400° until the cheese melts, about 8 minutes. This is a fun party treat for Halloween. Can be made ahead and frozen.

PLAY DOUGH

1 ½ cups salt
3 cups flour
6 Tbsp. cream of tartar
3 cups water
6 Tbsp. oil
Food coloring

Combine all ingredients in large saucepan. Color with food coloring. Mix well and stir over low heat until it feels like "play dough."

EGG YOLK PAINT
(for decorating sugar cookies)

1 egg yolk
¼ tsp. water
Food coloring

Blend well egg yolk and water. Divide mixture among cups in a muffin tin. Add a different food coloring to each cup to make bright colors. Paint designs on cookies with small paintbrushes. If the egg yolk paint thickens, add a few drops of water to thin.

Try removing crayon marks from the wall with toothpaste. It works great.

EQUIVALENT MEASURES

3 teaspoons = 1 tablespoon
16 tablespoons = 1 cup
2 cups = 1 pint
4 cups = 1 quart
2 pints = 1 quart
4 quarts (liquid) = 1 gallon
4 tablespoons = ¼ cup
5⅓ tablespoons = ⅓ cup
1 cup = 8 fluid ounces
pinch or dash is less than 1/8 teaspoon
2 tablespoons = 1 fluid ounce
1 pound = 16 ounces

Substitutions

1 tablespoon cornstarch (for thickening) = 2 tablespoon flour (approximately).

1 cup sifted all-purpose flour = 1 cup plus 2 tablespoons sifted cake flour.

1 square chocolate (oz.) = 3-4 tablespoons cocoa plus ½ tablespoon shortening.

1 teaspoon baking powder = ¼ teaspoon baking soda plus ½ teaspoon cream of tartar.

1 cup bottled milk = ½ cup evaporated milk plus ½ cup water.

1 cup sour milk = 1 cup sweet milk into which 1 tablespoon vinegar or lemon juice has been stirred; or 1 cup buttermilk.

1 cup sweet milk = 1 cup sour milk or buttermilk plus ½ teaspoon baking soda.

1 cup molasses = 1 cup honey.

1 cup sour cream = 1 cup evaporated milk plus 1 tablespoon vinegar or lemon juice.

1 whole egg = 2 egg yolks plus 1 tablespoon water (in cookies) or 2 egg yolks (in custards and similar mixtures).

1 tablespoon fresh herbs = 1 tsp. dry herbs.

1/8 teaspoon garlic powder = 1 small pressed clove of garlic.

1 cup fine crumbs = 24 saltine crackers, 4 slice breads, or 14 squares graham crackers.

INDEX

245

247

253